Questing for Understanding

Questing for Understanding

Persons, Places, Passions

David B. Burrell, CSC

 CASCADE *Books* · Eugene, Oregon

QUESTING FOR UNDERSTANDING
Persons, Places, Passions

Cascade Books
An Imprint of Wipf and Stock Publishers
199 W. 8th Ave., Suite 3
Eugene, OR 97401

www.wipfandstock.com

ISBN 13: 978-1-61097-686-2

Cataloging-in-Publication data:

Burrell, David B.

Questing for understanding : persons, places, passions / David B. Burrell.

viii + 122 p. ; 23 cm. —Includes bibliographical references.

ISBN 13: 978-1-61097-686-2

1. Burrell, David B. 2. Theologians—United States—Biography. I. Title.

BX4827.B90 P45 2012

Manufactured in the U.S.A.

These reflections, which owe so much to so many
and notably to my religious community,
are best dedicated to
Elena Malits, CSC,
in gratitude for her accompaniment

Encourage one another daily . . . to become partners of Christ, holding the beginning of the reality firm until the end.

Hebrews 3:13–14, NAB

Exhort one another every day . . . For we have become partners of Christ, if only we hold our first confidence firm to the end.

Hebrews 3:13–14, NRSV

Contents

Introduction

Orientations—Persons, Places, Passions

FOLLOWING THE ENCOURAGEMENT OF others, I offer this extended reflection on the life and times that have been mine. I hesitated to do so for some time, since that is not the sort of thing those of us called to serve others ever intended to do. Yet we are enjoined—thank God and the rule of the Congregation of Holy Cross—to set aside time each year for assessing our personal encounter with that God, so passing the three-quarter century mark on the first of March 2008 alerted me to the upheavals that have attended a life that long, so emboldened me to try to articulate them. I have always been chary of people who composed their story at a relatively early age, for only God knows what might ensue for them—*in sh'Allah!* The same could be true at seventy-five years, of course, but that mark has a way of bringing a recollected self to the fore. Yet while Augustine alerted us to the perils of such a venture, he also showed us how using what one recollects to praise God can be salutary for all. The very process of recollecting surfaces the trickster in us all, to remind us what tenuous and distorting access we have to ourselves: others will ever know us far better than we can know ourselves! So I have let these recollections emerge over time, returning to the specific places that have helped define me, amending the account each time. In that sense, reflections of this sort never end until we submit them to an editor; they remain revisable, a task that friends may continue after their publication.

So each of us becomes what mathematicians call a "point of accumulation," bringing the cross-currents of our times to a focus by the way we respond to them, appropriating them as we suffer them. Those privy to my annual Christmas letters over the decade at Tantur Ecumenical Institute in Jerusalem have become acutely aware of the transformation effected by suffering through the apparently intractable (if simply resolvable) conflict in the Holy Land. My own passage from endemic American optimism to an explicitly theological hope has been a painful one, brought about by the longsuffering of all who taught me to lay down the optimist's idiom of "coping" to suffer with them. If Tantur offers the most salient locale, the role it has played led me to identify my own passage in terms of places and people rather than simple chronology. Let us hope that pattern of people and places might help others profit from these reflections as well, for there can be no other point to composing them.

I am a lover, blessed from birth, it seems, by a propensity to love whatever I am engaged in. So whatever others may have called accomplishments were less goals sought than emergent passions forged by each engagement. In the narrative that follows I try to give due expression to this extraordinary gift. For such a propensity may be regarded as purely temperamental, which Aristotle called "natural virtue" since it requires little or no effort. In that vein, some have dubbed it "pathological optimism," but there is more to it: a gifted sense to discern what is worthy of love from what is not. Probably the fruit of a healthy family formation, it can hardly be that "natural" after all.

Yet this discerning sense is quite spontaneous, reflected in persons and endeavors to which I have been attracted. So we can only be grateful for something eluding explanation yet which has never ceased to keep me from self-destructing, as misjudgments in *eros* would invariably surface before capturing me. For as little as this can be accounted for, we might as well speak of a "guardian angel," as examples of caring cumulate, in circumstances small and great. I have learned from Arab friends—Christian or Muslim—to simply exclaim, "Alhamdulillah!": "May God be praised!" What else is there to say? As our Holy Cross ordination class celebrated fifty years of priesthood in 2010, I found myself parrying American expressions of "congratulations" by recalling that fifty years can hardly be regarded as an accomplishment; all is gift: "Alhamdulillah!"

Diverse ways of being a lover have emerged over time, as I learned to take heart from the valedictory observation of John of the Cross: "At the evening of our lives we shall be judged on love"—a lapidary summation of Matthew 25. The innate propensity to love anything in which I have been engaged ineluctably led to becoming an inveterate achiever, however, so the psyche was forced to administer the corrective of "falling in love." As we shall see, it was the gentle yet insistent therapy of a Jungian guide, Helen Luke, which led me to listen to the psyche to help discern among competing loves. So this narrative will monitor competing loves, attempting to articulate how each contributes to fashioning an ever more discerning lover, through one miscue after another, yet leading forward in sinuous ways: "Alhamdulillah!" Yet the achiever will not die, evidenced in a burning desire to seek the most notable promontory, to climb the highest mountain. So when obvious promontories were unavailable, others would be substituted. When asked at a relatively young age (thirty-eight) to chair the Department of Theology at Notre Dame, I also accepted a Routledge contract to undertake a contemporary study of Thomas Aquinas (in their Arguments of the Philosophers series), conscious of the need to keep honing habits of intellectual inquiry. These developed in undergraduate life at Notre Dame and were then fostered by our mentor in Rome, Bernard Lonergan, whom I tried to thank by putting his groundbreaking set of articles on "word in Aquinas" into book format, the result being *Verbum: Word and Idea in Aquinas* (1967). (His letter of appreciation noted more than a few typos!)

We shall explore the richness of the learning period afforded university administration in due time, but in retrospect the most telling countercurrent to administrative prowess was less the projected study of Aquinas as it was the spiritual mentorship of Helen Luke, whose community of Apple Farm (in Three Rivers, Michigan) will figure as a signal "station" among those stations in the inner journey that this itinerary singles out to articulate and celebrate. Yet engaging in university administration at one level can easily anticipate further levels to come, and in my case that prospect could easily titillate an achieving self by the prospect of becoming president of Notre Dame, a position reserved for members of the Congregation of Holy Cross. Three of us contemporaries were coming to be regarded (in the seventies) as promising candidates. Yet this proved less a distraction from administrative or intellectual work than it was an albatross, yet one from which events would liberate me to aspire to different heights. At the same time, however, generous and stimulating colleagues helped me maintain my focus on the tasks at hand, including Ernan McMullin, Stan Hauerwas, Joe Blenkinsopp, Robert Wilken, John Howard Yoder, among others, of whom more later. Finally, in following this story as it unfolds, the narrative will endeavor to honor Carl Jung's observation that the story of our lives will always be the story of our times.

Yet sensitivity to those times can be enhanced or blocked by the places we inhabit, so (for example) preoccupation with the stimulation of study in Rome in the late fifties effectively insulated me from world-shaping events in Hungary at the same time. So close yet so far! The unyielding linkage between place and time would lead me to seek to be in the right place at the right time, giving the impression of a peripatetic life when travel became more feasible. I have been unable to resist calls to be in what seemed to be the right place at the right time, so these opportunities invariably expanded my appreciation of the human dimension of the events taking place. Invariably these displacements have nourished an intellectual desire better to understand, using them to learn the language of the place, the better to meet people whose lives displayed what that place had to teach. As a result, I am a poor tourist, bored looking at the outside of monumental buildings, yearning rather to be invited into a family for tea. So I am grateful that I can now enjoy a number of "destinations," whose call keeps me from needing to travel elsewhere. I relish sharing those persons and places again and again.

Yet while Jung never ceases to remind us that the story of our lives will always be the story of our times, he insisted as well that it remains our task to discover how that is the case, and how that story renders people and places significant. So a personal story can never be one's own. At the outset of a new phase of life, in service to the Holy Cross district of East Africa, it seemed fitting to follow the suggestion of many friends to compose "my story." Family comes first and looms large in setting out to trace the genealogy of becoming the lover I have become. Reared ecumenically by an English Catholic mother and a Scottish Presbyterian father, whose mother had had him baptized Anglican in Montana, my life was tracked by these realities, but in a different key from most American Catholics, whose ecclesial affiliations were often ethnic: Irish, Italian, German, or Irish-Italian ("Itralian"). Ours was less dramatic, more Anglo-Saxon, yet on arriving in Rome to study theology in 1956 at twenty-three, I would realize how uptight and Waspish were my sensibilities, though now mysteriously ripe for immersion in Latin culture. As students at the University of Notre Dame, some of us had already been primed by the witness of a Holy Cross priest, born in Germany, who had studied theology in France in the thirties, and who had alerted us to intercultural exposure. The following four years would also prepare us for the Second Vatican Council, beginning five years later, whose fresh air we welcomed, for it confirmed the superior education we received at the Gregorian in the late fifties. In the summer of 1958, I would make final vows in the Congregation of Holy Cross in the German-speaking Südtirol region of Italy, only to be ordained to the priesthood in Rome a year and half later, with my parents as witnesses.

Upon completing undergraduate studies at Notre Dame I had drifted into the Congregation nearly by default. Increasingly haunted by the thought that the Lord might want me to serve God's people as a priest, I had relished the intellectual milieu of the newfound General Program of Liberal Studies, modeled on the fabled College of the University of Chicago. Yet in the end I was moved mysteriously to turn down two fellowships for graduate study in Europe to cast my lot with Holy Cross, keenly sensing that it was now or never to follow up the nagging thought of serving God as a priest. (No telling whom I might meet in Europe!) The witness of Holy Cross priests at Notre Dame had hardly proved stellar to us, but I followed the witness of the German-American mentor just mentioned, Louis J. Putz, CSC. He had always exhibited gratitude to a community that allowed him to be and to act as unusually and creatively as he did. Knowing how to stroke a young man's ego, he gently reminded me, "You have learned a lot at Notre Dame!" I probably also needed to distinguish myself from the Saint Louis family of my mother, replete with Jesuits, as well as a few experiences with American Dominicans, who invariably presented themselves as possessing "the truth," which portended a very dull life.

Serendipitously, I was before long to find a family in Holy Cross, whose nineteenth-century founder, Basil Moreau, intended it to be a microcosm of church: male and female, lay and clerical. I soon came to feel that he masked the radicality of this prospect even from himself by the pious image of the "holy family"—priests as Jesus, sisters as Mary, and brothers as Joseph. Yet it proved a pregnant image as well. In the 1850s Rome did not permit a canonical mix of men and women, yet as the church has become sensitized to the need always to present a male and female face, our familial structure came gradually to fulfillment, especially in Asia, Africa, and South America. In North America, the astounding "success" of religious communities engaged in education and health care in the early twentieth century certainly helped Catholics make an imprint in a resolutely Protestant society, yet these very works tended as well to segregate men from women into single-sex institutions. A stint in Bangladesh (in 1975) would confirm my attraction to Holy Cross, as I discovered how fruitfully men and women can cooperate in doing God's work, as we now experience in the East African context as well.

The perspective granted by Holy Cross will accentuate some key realities of my life and times in the Catholic Church. Noting how the original vision of Basil Moreau was eclipsed for a time—only to emerge in the culture fostered by the renewal of Vatican II—indicates how a person's lifetime can be intimately intertwined with history in the making. The educational and academic dimension of my life remains to be fleshed out, with its own startling evolutions, where an interfaith world will flower as professional and religious realities conspired to elicit a transforming response. Those dimensions then converged with my Holy Cross community to direct me to Africa, where the dire consequences of a Western-directed globalization forcibly accentuate other sociopolitical realities, much as a decade in the Holy Land would presage American misadventures in Iraq. In each setting, experiencing the effects of colonization has sorely reminded me how we "Westerners" cannot but represent colonizing powers. Assimilating that inescapable fact while learning proper ways to respond to it will be part of the transformation these years have effected.

The original gift from my religious congregation of theological study in Rome, followed twenty years later by the gift of a semester in Bangladesh, set a pattern of reflective distance from American origins, leading to ongoing critical assessment of our country's presence in the world. Holy Cross presence in Chile and Peru had sensitized us to "liberation theology" as well, irrevocably establishing how Christian faith is inseparable from sociopolitical realities. Indeed, any retreat from that realization can only be a self-serving denial of the way Jesus' own life manifests the intertwining of faith and life in the world. So the decades that my own life has spanned have reminded us all how lives make statements as well, as key protagonists of liberation theology have given ultimate witness to their grasp of the truth of the gospel, as did Martin Luther King and Mohandas Gandhi during this same epoch.

While a perspective of seventy-five years encourages one to identify certain junctures as decisive, the journey that transformed an American destined to be a priest-professor at Notre Dame into an inquirer nourished by Judaism and Islam, one at home in the Mediterranean world of West Asia (Jerusalem) after immersion in the Muslim milieu of South Asia (Bangladesh), and now East Africa, suggested a way to organize the story geographically rather than chronologically. For in fact we do not live our lives serially according to distinct periods of time; we rather live them in places suffused with overlapping temporal perspectives as well. This indisputable fact seems better limned in my case by a geographical palimpsest, illustrating how the overlay of diverse cultures nourishes a life lived in the present. Although enculturation into these distinct places took place at a particular time, within a distinct period of my life, their shaping significance remains, as they each contributed to forging this particular lover.

Friends with whom we have once bonded continue to enrich the person we have become, so we find ourselves taking up the conversation wherever we left it off, whenever we encounter one another again. Grasping how Augustine's *Confessions* were oriented by friendships helped me appreciate the way friends can open the times we share into fruitful venues. Friendship frees us to call upon one another to negotiate the travails of our times, so the name of the game is "juxtapositions." Freud relied heavily upon the term in his "talk therapy," showing how revealing spontaneous juxtapositions can prove to be. A chronological account at first presents itself as more reasonable, until we realize that we don't live our lives that way. So in fact a geographical approach appears more illuminating, for it highlights the ways we encounter realities and allow them to shape us. And in most cases, places embody family connections, whether with natural or religious families, and so have enabled me to become rooted in different regions and cultures, by familial origins or through relationships inspired by the family of Holy Cross, or by a variety of professional encounters.

This strategy will also allow me (after an "origins" chapter) to begin with the present, and with Africa. I first encountered this continent in 1975, en route from Jerusalem to Dhaka to serve in Bangladesh, on a symbolic journey, as I saw it then, from Judaism to Islam. So at the outset Africa formed a bridge to Asia for me, even if that journey had begun in West Asia. (Ironically, we continue to refer to that part of the world as "Middle East," even though it is only "east" or "middle" from London.) Both geographically and culturally, via the institution of slaving, Africa links Asia with North and South America. It also undergirds that peninsula of Asia that we name "Europe," across a sea named for its median position between three continents, both separating and connecting them in ways that would later lead me into a fresh understanding of medieval philosophical developments.

Once I came to realize the inherent connection between "Catholic" and "Italian," my fate was sealed; despite northern European origins I became a Mediterranean person. Though readily at home in western Europe, my heart fixed on the Mediterranean basin, so a preternatural draw to that region would effectively anticipate ten years' presence in the Holy Land. Yet the fascination with difference—different languages and practices, different skin hues and dress, different ways of approaching and understanding reality—had begun with studies in Rome. That arc would then move from West Asia to the Asian subcontinent, and later to Iran, and from all of these to Africa. Yet among peoples whom we call "Africans," there are countless differences, for the very name is a European construction of the nineteenth century, when the Berlin Conference (1884–85) carved up a continent in order to exploit it. So "Africa" can only name a continent, not a culture, as the continent embraces countless cultures.

Yet there is one culture that links Africa with Asia. Often it is not reckoned with Africa, yet Egypt fairly represents the axis of this Mediterranean world. Thinking with Freud and Foucault of the "archaeology of the spirit," we find three layers of civilization in Egypt: Pharaonic, Coptic Christian, and Muslim—a palimpsest. There I was introduced into Arabic, discovering a Thomas Aquinas virtually ignored by scholars far more erudite than I. This natively Mediterranean Aquinas found inspiration for his border crossings from a Jewish rabbi writing in Arabic, Moses ben Maimon (Maimonides). Fastening upon his *The Guide for the Perplexed* as soon as it was rendered into Latin, Aquinas used its key strategies to bolster his own. Even while their respective revelation-traditions had by then become quite alien to each other, their goal was identical. Both sought to free persons of faith to do philosophy, as well as to show how philosophical strategies can illuminate revelation. And though fifty years separated the lifetimes of these two scholars from one another, a shared Mediterranean culture brought them into contact.

Having completed a study of Aquinas along Western lines (1979), my locus of learning shifted in the decades following to the Dominican Institute for Oriental Studies, with its resident guru, Georges Anawati, OP. Already a legend in his time, he gave ample attention to middle-aged neophytes like myself in search of ways to bridge the worlds astride which he so gracefully stood like the Colossus of Rhodes. The community that he had founded (at the end of World War II), and that sustained him throughout his scholarly and priestly life, found in him a gentle and faithful older brother. Although we tended to refer to him as "Abouna" ("our father"), Dominicans regularly call one another "brother," and in this diverse community, situated at the intellectual heart of the Muslim world a few kilometers from al-Azhar, brothers care singularly for one another.

So this special place, Cairo, connected me with another religious community, one that adopted me as a "corresponding member." Within contexts of shared faith like these, intimate friendships can be nourished, as the culture we share links us to our creator and to one another. I have often reflected on the manifold blessings of this unique form of fellowship that allows one to be welcomed into a strange city in a home formed by regular prayer and replete with intellectual and spiritual exchange. (By contrast, hotels can be cold and off-putting, the more so as they try to mask impersonality with luxuries.) So members of Catholic religious communities are especially privileged; I call it "letting celibacy work for us!" All this allowed Cairo, Hania in Crete, and Jerusalem to triangulate the eastern Mediterranean for me. So it is immaterial which came first, though it was in fact Jerusalem. For each of these places reinforces the other, as Jerusalem, Athens, and Cairo readily symbolize the Jewish, Christian, Muslim world that a quarter-century of study has made my home. But as we shall see, only friends make a place a home: in this case, a passel of friends in the Jerusalem area, a Notre Dame classmate in Hania (in Crete) who claimed his Cretan-Muslim and Turkish-Jewish heritage in the mid-sixties, and Dominican brothers in Cairo. So people far more embedded in these cultures than I could ever hope to be became my mentors in each place, palpably enriching my life and humbling me by their erudition and simplicity, with their ready welcome of a brother, often across demarcations of faiths. Without friends like these, I could never have dreamt to undertake the border crossings that will punctuate these reflections.

Five groupings will comprise the axial places around which these chapters turn: (1) initial grounding in family life and student days at Notre Dame, followed by (2) Rome, then (3) higher studies leading to forty-two years at Notre Dame, with alternate academic sites in Bangladesh, Hyde Park, and Cambridge; (4) the Holy Land, Cairo and Crete; then (5) Apple Farm in Three Rivers, Michigan, and the Sisters of Loretto

Motherhouse in Nerinx, Kentucky, followed by an epilogue bringing us to East Africa. Rome (2) proves to be as axial as family and Notre Dame, introducing me into diverse cultures and languages, as well as a refined understanding of faith, while (3) depicts Notre Dame as the longest axial locus, constantly enriched by (4) crossing boundaries and centuries to open mind and heart to intellectual and personal interfaith exchange, and (5) introducing gender complementarity in an abiding quest for fidelity to spiritual seeking. The chapter that brings us to East Africa will also focus on friendships to serve as a valedictory act of gratitude. So let us now track the chronology leading to these axial places, to try to show the shaping role each of them will play in forging the lover I have become.

1

Origins

Grounding in Family with a Fresh Foundation at Notre Dame

BEGINNING WITH FAMILY AND with Notre Dame reminds us how indispensable chronology remains, to acknowledge how formative is family, as well as to emphasize how the Notre Dame ethos turns on an instinct for family, usually quite positively yet sometimes exploitatively. Indeed, its pattern of residentiality works as well as it does when students have gained familial skills at home. Encountering a dear friend in a Benedictine monastery during a cross-country drive only to ask him how his retreat was going, he had to admit: "Sixty-five and one is still on the 'mother thing.'" A skilled director of the "exercises" of Saint Ignatius and a brutally honest man, this friend knew that family never leaves us, much as parenting never ceases, so tracing familial interaction can be a fruitful form of therapy in later life. It is especially fascinating to try to trace what shaped the lover in me. Like so many Americans, my parents conveyed a mixed heritage: mother from a Catholic family prominent in Saint Louis, with English, Scottish, and French roots (via Guadalupe planters), with the Scottish side boasting the first governor of Missouri while the English side carried the Bakewell name from Derbyshire. Conversion to Catholicism in the Oxford movement in mid-nineteenth century moved our great-grandfather (Robert Armitage Bakewell) from Congregational minister to editor of the Catholic newspaper in Saint Louis. His son, my grandfather, served as first dean of the Saint Louis University Law School while practicing as a patent attorney. Of his children with Eugenia McNair, my mother came near the end, close to a sister who died quite young, three older brothers, who became (in order) a respected estate lawyer, a real estate tycoon, and a Jesuit who died prematurely shortly before ordination, with one older sister whom we never came to know. A family replete with distinction and mutual respect, but quite reticent to show love.

The parents of my father, Roger Burrell, had moved to Montana from Illinois, where his father, Alexander, had become a mining engineer in the coalfields of Illinois, marrying Abigail Kiersted, whose mother had been Bridget Kelly. With the endorsement of a cousin, Bill Chalmers (of Chalmers and Williams, later Allis-Chalmers), Alexander Burrell was selected to oversee British capitalization of a fresh gold strike in Marysville (outside Helena) before the turn of the century. The mine—the Drum Lummond—produced for some twenty years, allowing my grandfather to distinguish himself in the fledgling mining industry, make annual trips to England to report to the stockholders, and serve in the early Montana legislature. After the mine "played out," Abigail encouraged her husband to move the family to a ranch near Choteau, which my father took to enthusiastically, managing a three thousand acre cattle ranch in high school, while his father continued to serve as consultant to western mining properties. Drawn by whatever sirens to enroll in the American Field Service early in the First World War—the "Great War" to Europeans—he served as a noncombatant ambulance driver for the entire sweep of the conflict. Only later (in Sebastian Faulks' *Birdsong*) was I exposed to accounts of the horrors of trench warfare, which our father never recounted to us.

His greatest disappointment on returning was that his older brothers had lost the ranch in the volatile times following that war, for my father had intended to make a go of it. He never lost his love for "the West," however, celebrated by periodic visits to A. B. ("Bud") Guthrie Jr. at the University of Kentucky, whose novels (*The Way West, The Big Sky*) limned panoramically the world of Choteau, where his father had been local schoolmaster. Necessity forced my father to find work elsewhere, so his cousin Bill Chalmers engaged him to sell mining machinery in Québec, where he could use his newfound French. Traveling through Saint Louis to sell machinery to the Desloge lead mines in Missouri (in 1922), my father contacted an American Field Service buddy, who serendipitously introduced him to the woman who would become our mother.

Nancy Bakewell's family status placed her in the socialite stratum, but she had managed to escape its ethos by working for Catholic Relief Services in Washington DC after the war, hosted by Maria Ewing (of the Sherman-Ewing family), who became a lifelong friend. By the time she met my father for lunch, she had taken the measure of three other men (to whom she had been briefly engaged) to know her mind and heart. So she accepted his proposal when he returned barely a month later. Roughly Roger Burrell's age, Nancy had been as adventurous as was permitted to a woman of her class at the time, while Roger had broken horses in Montana and tended to the wounded and removed corpses from trenches in France. One can only speculate that the further adventure of leaving sedate Saint Louis society with a "man of the world" who was not Catholic appealed to my mother's sense of adventure. They left for New York, where his elder brother, John Angus Burrell, was teaching English at Columbia, and where their first son was born, until lured by an offer of work in Akron, Ohio, where my father would soon become advertising director of John Knight's first newspaper, the *Akron Beacon Journal*. In a locale hardly equal to the adventures just sketched, and culturally backward to my mother, they quickly became absorbed in family—four boys and a girl—while the newspaper position saw the family through the Great Depression and proved a stable base during the Second World War, in which our oldest brother served as a medic with the fleet marines on many Pacific landings, with the next in naval officer training when hostilities ceased.

What I recall of our life together was its shape and its quality. We were taught to be different, with a touch of faith and of aristocracy from our mother, complemented by tolerant, astute judgment on the part of our father. Their witness and mutual respect taught us to respect one another and others as well, with "consideration for others" as the watchword. The result was a secure nest spiced with an impulse to explore the world, as our ecumenical parents assured that we were raised in an atmosphere of tolerance and critical thinking. My three older brothers—Alan, Alec, and Paul—were born in 1924, 1926, and 1928, respectively, so formed a close cohort. They grew up during the Depression, but my father's position as advertising manager of the *Akron Beacon Journal* apparently insulated the family from privation, depriving them at most, my brothers told me, of ice cream! Moreover, in the summer of 1938 my father was able to send them all to camp in Colorado, so that his sons—aged fourteen, twelve, and ten—could taste the mountains he treasured so much. He would joke about the modest fees of Camp Saint Malo, suggesting it was cheaper to send three growing boys there for a month than to feed them at home! Not quite, of course, yet he wanted them to experience the expansive land that had made him and from which he had been exiled. That fateful lunch in Saint Louis had turned him into a spouse, father, and householder, and he never looked back. It would take eight years and a world war before I was deemed old enough to go to Camp Saint Malo, yet we shall see the powerful effect of those summers and learn more of that singular camp. I was to accompany my parents on two trips west after that, allowing Dad to reminisce about life on the ranch in ways palpable and poignant.

In the meantime, my sister Nina and I formed a "second family," as my older brothers went away for high school—Alan to Portsmouth Priory in Rhode Island, Alec and Paul to Campion in Prairie du Chein, Wisconsin. So the trails they blazed were often remote from our lives, yet I looked up to them inestimably—especially Alan, older by nine years, which rendered him "grown-up" in my eyes. Moreover, he was what one calls "a natural"—good at whatever he did, excelling in sports, studies, and with girls. The prep school he attended was guided by monks from Ampleforth Abbey in England and designed to appeal to eastern Catholics' desire to excel in a WASP world; the students, given a Catholic formation, would be directed to Ivy League universities. Yet the monks kept an austere profile, housing students in spartan quarters with religious oversight, as a counterpoint to the wealthy families from which many of them came. The ethos of an English "public school"—consummately private, in fact—tended to prevail over American inclinations to conspicuous consumption. Such a local ethos must have facilitated Alan's integration into that society, for he was a scholarship student, negotiated by Maria Ewing, my mother's indomitable friend from her Washington work in Catholic Relief after the war. Yet Alan's natural talent for everything the school and his fellow students valued must have brought him universal appreciation, so he felt no need to compete in income status. Predilection for boarding school was less a matter of status than of my mother's convictions from a Saint Louis background with Jesuit educators, leading her to prefer men to teach her sons, while the best Akron could muster were Dominican sisters.

Named for his father, Roger Allen Burrell, but using Dad's middle name with a variant spelling, Alan graduated from Portsmouth Priory in June 1941, entering the University of Virginia as a freshman in the fall in which World War II began. My father counseled prudence, strongly suggesting that he wait to be drafted, but Alan followed Dad's example rather than his advice, enlisting in the Navy at the end of the academic year 1941–42. Inducted immediately into officer training, it was not long before he told an officious "officer of the day" to "go to hell" and was "busted" to boot camp outside Chicago, where he entered medic training, to be assigned to the fleet marines for most of the Pacific landings, attending the wounded much as his father had. An avid correspondent and talented writer—another "natural"—on "liberty" before leaving he worked out a code to elude the military censors and tell us where he was: the first letter of the word beginning each paragraph would spell his location.

The next member of the cohort, Alexander McNair, was named after his paternal grandfather, Alexander Burrell, as well as our mother's Scottish ancestor, Alexander McNair, who had been the first governor of Missouri. An achiever from the beginning, doubtless to compensate for his elder's abundant talents, he excelled in the Jesuit environment of Campion Preparatory School, largely populated by relatively well-off boys from Chicago, but hardly the affluent eastern set Alan had had to negotiate. On graduation he was swept up into naval officer training, assigned to a nearby college in Ohio for study and training until the war ended, leaving him the solitary claim of having fought "the battle of Baldwin-Wallace"—the name of the college. He went on to become an advertising agency executive with dreams of affluence, but that hard-driving, hard-drinking life did not serve him or his family well, and after a serious bout of sclerosis of the liver, he moved valiantly into food banking, using his marketing skills to serve the poor in Saint Louis, where the family had settled, with their three daughters in Sacred Heart schools. His wife, Helen Louise Vaughn, had been adopted into an affluent Akron family, yet did not hesitate to use her considerable sewing skills to help alleviate the drop in family income. Alec was the first to die, and suddenly so, from an aortic aneurism with no warning, at seventy-four.

The third boy, Paul Bakewell, was named after mother's father, a distinguished patent attorney in Saint Louis and a prominent Catholic, serving as first dean of St. Louis University Law School. (His son, McNair, my mother's younger brother, would enter the Jesuits, only to die prematurely in his twenties while serving at Campion as a "scholastic.") My brother, Paul, however, was hardly suited to the military mien of the "company of

Jesus." Sent to Campion after his brother Alec, they had overlapped only one year when Paul took "French leave," hopping a Burlington freight train to Saint Louis with another "misfit." Like most rebels of that age, however, he soon sought the refuge of his Uncle Bud, himself a prominent attorney like his father, who alerted our father, so Dad took the train to Saint Louis to fetch him. So ended my mother's burning desire to have her sons educated by religious men, as Paul completed his high school in the Akron public system, then going on to study at the college at Columbia University, where our Uncle John had taught all his life. He had shown himself to be different, and would fulfill that the rest of his life. We were four years apart in school, so when Dad drove me east to look at colleges in the fall of 1945, staying with Uncle John in his apartment on the Upper West Side, Paul was reluctant for Dad to see the quarters he had rented after moving out of the dorms. But Dad insisted, so we walked together to a bohemian efficiency, where the latest coat of paint could hardly have been worse. Paul did not even resent Dad's remarking, "When are you moving?" for he had to admit that reading Dostoyevsky in that setting could be depressing.

Paul's voracious intellectual desires clearly destined him for university life and teaching in the humanities, yet I suspect that the life he experienced, folded into Uncle John's faculty soirées, led him to try a more ordinary route first. So he returned to Akron after Columbia to take a job in the office of a trucking firm but trained to be a driver and "pulled freight" to and from New York for two years. The experience of the road and his cohort probably taught him more than a Columbia education and subsequent pursuit of doctoral studies combined, while his presence in Akron at that time—clearly the last place he wanted to be—led to meeting a talented pianist (through our mother's offices) who would become his wife and the mother of their children. Rachel Ober shared many of Paul's distinctive values, to the point where my father regularly said that "their marriage saved two others." In the sixties, Paul and Rachel introduced racial integration into their elementary school in Cincinnati, where Paul had taken his first (and only) faculty position, teaching French at the university. They loved the German-Jewish milieu, for its parks and music, yet resisting all the while the local newspaper's bourgeois mindset. Paul was a devotee of secondhand bookshops and clothing stores; in fact, Paul and Rachel's shared animosity to a consumer society led them invariably to everything "secondhand," instilling that penchant in their children. (We shall remark the transformation worked in the life of this family in 1982, when David, their eldest, was killed on a bicycle, at twenty-seven years old.)

As the one closest to me, my brother Paul introduced me to life as a boy. He was a natural explorer, more of a loner than I, yet neither of us took to team sports. We rather went hiking in the woods behind our house, through which two rail lines and a river ran. We built forts and shelters, and as we grew older, used bows and arrows and 22-caliber rifles to hit targets; the most fun was to try to shatter bottles thrown into the river. (Our father had taught his sons three skills a western man needed: to carve meat, mix drinks, and use firearms safely.) As a result I tended to be odd man out in high school, where football, basketball, and baseball reigned supreme. I did help start a tennis team for our Catholic high school, which is hardly a team sport.

When our brothers returned home from the military, they interceded with mother for Nina and me to remain home for high school, so she relented once she had elicited from the Dominican sisters the promise that I would be able to complete four years of Latin! My sister would spend her first two years with those same sisters in Akron, whereupon the pull of the Sacred Heart education that our mother had enjoyed led Nina to complete high school at Villa Duchesne in Saint Louis, which in her case proved enriching and life-sustaining. Christmas vacations, however, allowed us both to participate in a cohort of friends in Akron who continue to grace our lives—few in number but rich in quality. Nina developed intimate relationships with two girls who were bereft of brothers, gaining sisters for herself and giving the others access to male companions as well, while our own relationship unfolded in miraculous ways as our separate lives came to enrich one another.

When I confided to my father at the end of high school that I felt called, perhaps, to serve God as a priest, his immediate response was, "What you do with your life is your business, but I wish you would go to college first." No doubt he feared undue influence on someone so young in a seminary context, yet what I felt then was his unstinting support, and in retrospect immense gratitude for the vistas that a creative undergraduate program in "great books" was to open to me at Notre Dame. In short, he was right; seminary education would have been far more confining, intellectually as well as emotionally, at that age. I had a penchant for fixing things, so when I wanted to use some of my paper route earnings to purchase a motor scooter in the last year of high school, my mother was clearly terrified as mothers should indeed be, but my father simply suggested that I would probably learn a lot from the experience of purchasing, driving, and repairing it—which I did, for three months.

Given the independent yet responsible shape of our father's youth, he was inclined to let us learn from experience, encouraging us to assess it ourselves, always willing to offer another perspective yet never overwhelming us with advice. Indeed, I have often remarked how the conventional gender complementarity was quite reversed in our family, with a mother more demanding and ambitious for us, and a father to whom we could readily turn when we failed to meet her mark. Clearly he showed me the way to become the lover I am.

Certainly our father must have felt that he was "camping out" in Akron as much as mother, who never failed to remark that "all of Akron needs a coat of paint!" But for quite different reasons; my father missed the West, especially Montana. For a time he kept a horse in a stable nearby, but the riding paths in the Cuyahoga Valley must have seemed tame to one who had been a forest ranger in the Flathead National Forest, and who at one point "ran out" two horses to be with his dying mother. So he jumped at the chance to send my three older brothers to camp in Colorado in 1938. Located near Estes Park on the front range of the Rockies—the same range that my father's family had faced in Choteau, Montana—Camp Saint Malo was a low-budget, high-activity camp directed by Monsignor Bosetti, vicar general of the diocese of Denver and a lover of the mountains, something he instilled in all the boys. Accommodations were basic: one dorm with a hundred campers monitored by a few seminarians, cold showers, and a swimming pool fed by mountain streams. My brothers loved it, so I could not wait to go, but the war intervened. So I had to wait until 1946, when my oldest brother returned from the Pacific to sign on as a counselor, with my brother Paul as a "worker," and I as a camper.

Uncle John joined my father from New York to drive us there, enduring the vast Nebraska plains until mountains claimed the horizon. Father Bosetti regularly hosted Vatican staff from the apostolic delegation in Washington, so the "head table" included our father, Uncle John, Monsignor Bosetti, Monsignor Lardoni (apostolic delegate to Canada), and Monsignor Ferrofino (from the Vatican delegation in Washington). Father Bosetti deemed French to be the common language, so we campers were treated to a table of adults conversing in French in the Rockies! That summer and the next confirmed my love for the mountains, while daily eucharistic celebrations in the exquisite "chapel on the rock" palpably nudged me towards the thought (at least) of becoming a priest. The mountains became part of me, and would remain so until one day thirty-five years later, on a visit to Bossy in Switzerland when the Alps, sparkling in the sun after a week of rain had washed the air clear, seemed all too much like a picture postcard. After six months in Jerusalem the desert had claimed my psyche, but until then it had been the mountains, thanks to summers at Camp Saint Malo.

Persistently excelling in high school, I thought of pursuing engineering, given my penchant for making things, and Notre Dame was one of the few Catholic colleges to have an engineering school. The summer I was accepted, however, Notre Dame announced a new program in "great books," modeled after the college program at the University of Chicago: the General Program of Liberal Education, an integral, four-year experiment in learning. Our favorite uncle, John, was visiting us from Columbia University when I received the brochure in the mail. He remarked my enthusiasm and confirmed that such an opportunity could hardly be overlooked, thrilled as he was that a Catholic university would move in the direction in which he had helped guide Columbia.

Whenever our parents wanted to reward us for something special, they would send us to New York to stay with Uncle John, who would meet us at the door of his Upper West Side flat, greet us warmly, and press subway tokens in our hands, saying, "I'll see you tonight." Entrusted to his care by our parents, we were given free rein of the city! Unmarried, John modeled "uncle" for us, showing me how to be one for twenty-one nieces and nephews, especially those who would study at Notre Dame. His attitudes towards Catholicism were of the critical academic variety, though he came to love and respect our mother, whose training in Sacred Heart schools prepared her to parry his barbs. We were later to appreciate that he was also our "gay uncle," though that language was hardly in vogue at the time. What we did notice, however, was his genius for cultivating and sustaining friendships. In 1956, Uncle John joined my parents and my brother Alec as we seminarians departed from New York to Naples on the USS Constitution. Since his wartime commission in the US Navy had been validated in the merchant marine, Uncle John was able to introduce us to the ship's captain, who promptly extended the favor to include his niece en route to Florence for study, assuring us access to a group of Fulbright students for the rest of the voyage.

Given the five years that separated our three older brothers from my sister Nina and me—just eighteen months apart—all of my brothers had married and left Akron by the time I completed college, with their spouses and families enriching and extending our family in quite different ways. (Some of their children would later come to study at Notre Dame once I began to teach there, giving me privileged access to those nieces and nephews.) But the immediate joy was to have more sisters, for my brothers' spouses were welcomed into the heart of our family. The year after college, while I was in the initiatory year in the Holy Cross family, my sister married, and the contrast was unfortunate, since for whatever complex reasons he did not fit in as the other spouses. Since they came to live two hours from South Bend in Grand Rapids, Michigan, I regularly visited the family while it was expanding to seven, the children growing rapidly, as children do. Nina stayed in the marriage until all but one had begun their college years, some at Notre Dame, by which time she had gained the inner courage to face the inevitable. A church annulment confirmed that their marriage, though it had produced seven remarkable children, often reared nearly single-handedly by my sister, could not continue as a relationship. Some fifteen years later, she was to marry a widower, the husband she always wanted, and was welcomed into his extended family.

Three of us siblings remain from our generation, with one sister-in-law and a rich diversity in the generations that follow. Our eldest brother Alan's family initiated inclusive annual reunions at the beach in North Carolina, where his daughter Nina lives with her family, so that diverse generations came to experience family. These events proved serendipitous for Alan and Katie's family, for the next generation's families had either boys or girls, so the annual reunion allowed boys to gain sisters, and girls, brothers. Yet to return to Paul, as I began to compose this story, I was journeying from Uganda to Cincinnati to celebrate the remarkable life of Paul's widow, Rachel, whose body expired at eighty while her spirit continues to live among us. Their eldest son, David, had been instantly killed on a bicycle at twenty-seven years old in 1982, now thirty years ago. Both parents had done all they could to "minister to" their children in the wake of it, yet Rachel took a further step to organize a center for grieving children, Fernside, in Cincinnati, where Paul served as the "pizza man." When he contracted Alzheimer's at sixty-five, the family gathered to support one another, and with their extensive experience with end-of-life situations, wisely determined "no intervention." So he died from pneumonia on 01/01/01, celebrated as an imaginative professor of French at the University of Cincinnati, yet perhaps better known as Rachel's husband.

Notre Dame Years

Leaving Akron, Ohio, for college in effect expanded my sense of family to embrace a superior education, replete with a prescient religious formation at Notre Dame, guided by a group inspired by Louis Putz, CSC, called Young Christian Students (YCS). Louis Putz had been introduced into this Belgian movement during his sojourn in France in the thirties, and he brought their unique formation scheme to Notre Dame when he made a stunning exit from France (still carrying a German passport) in the early days of the war, on one of the last passenger vessels to cross the Atlantic in 1939. The only moderately radical Catholic group in the fifties, YCS attracted exceptional people, providing an ecclesial formation that presaged Vatican II, and nourishing friendships that have continued to this day. The most salient of these for me has been Elena Malits, a Saint Mary's YCS student who became a Holy Cross sister herself, allowing our friendship to flourish for more than fifty years. Others will appear as the story unfolds, with Tesse and Bill Donnelly, their six children, and then their children, offering an exemplary scenario of friendship in faith. Fascinatingly, YCS emerges from this perspective as the most formative influence during my student years at Notre Dame, though our education there was exemplary. As the initial class of the General Program of Liberal Education, inaugurated by the president, John Cavanaugh, CSC, in the spirit of the collegiate education at the University of Chicago in "great books," spearheaded by his friend, John Maynard Hutchins, we were immersed in the classics of Western civilization. Regular seminars, together with tutorials using classics of mathematical and physical sciences to introduce those disciplines, introduced us into a carefully structured education with an immense range of freedom to explore within it.

Conventional terms could describe it as a program in philosophy and mathematics, but major credit goes to the sterling professors who guided us. Moreover, as I would later take up graduate studies in philosophy at

Yale, I found that I had read virtually all of those to whom professors referred, while many of my colleagues had but heard the names. With stimulating discussions among ourselves and rich interaction with faculty, many of us emerged with a compelling desire to carry on a life of inquiry. In our first weeks of class, when I offered a catechism-type response to a question, the priest leading our seminar retorted, "Why?"—thus launching us into a life of inquiry. Ours was a dramatic alternative to the standard fare in the College of Arts and Letters at Notre Dame, especially in philosophy and in theology, while other students took philosophy as well as "religion," the latter with notably subpar instructors. So we came to consider ourselves a cut above the others, hanging out when we could in Hyde Park (at the University of Chicago), though in retrospect the plebeian atmosphere of Notre Dame may have provided a healthy balance to our intellectual élan. Summer YCS "study weeks" at different college campuses confirmed the quality of this classical education, as we joined with students of varied educational formation and experience to probe ways of understanding the sociopolitical situation surrounding us, trying to diagnose it in light of the gospel. Our education may indeed have sharpened the diagnostics, yet we found ourselves considerably enhanced by exchanges during these precious weeks. It was there that my friendship with Tesse Hartigan began, a student from Fontbonne College in Saint Louis who had given two years of her life to be a "full-time worker" at YCS headquarters in the Chicago Loop, and then went on to the College of New Rochelle. I admired her ability to bring analytic tools to bear on contemporary situations.

In fact, many students whom we met at study weeks had backgrounds less sheltered and more adventuresome than mine, adding spice to these learning experiences. I had become enthralled with philosophy and adept at mathematics, and began to presume I would spend the rest of my life in an academic milieu; yet pure academics never appealed to me, despite and perhaps because Notre Dame had a few who so aspired. YCS had initiated me into dimensions of faith and of activism that have never diminished. As our final (senior) year progressed, I applied for Fulbright and Woodrow Wilson fellowships to study philosophy in Europe, yet had also to honor the inchoate yet insistent "call" to the priesthood. So in the spring of 1954 I spent Holy Week at Saint John's Monastery in Collegeville, Minnesota, where we had enjoyed a YCS study week the summer before. I had felt some stirring towards monastic life during that study week, and the mini-retreat afforded welcome distance from Notre Dame. I was able to speak with the abbot, doubtless hoping to impress him with the thought of "becoming a Benedictine." He wasted no time disabusing me: one did not "become a Benedictine" but rather joined a monastery. Taken aback, I pondered this on the way back on the train, concluding that nothing had prepared me to spend the rest of my life in northern Minnesota. It might well have been fine, but that rebuff returned me to Notre Dame and effectively to Holy Cross.

It must be said, however, that our group of seniors had little respect for the priests who lived with us in the residence halls, enforcing a French *lycée* regime, but of course our superior education left us with little respect for anyone other than our classmates and teachers in the General Program. So I had to be circumspect discussing Holy Cross with my friends. The key again was Louis Putz, who had always respected my freedom, never treating me as a "vocation prospect." Reporting about Saint John's, I timidly asked him, "What would you think of Holy Cross (for me)?" knowing how he loved his community, even while ever testing its boundaries. Knowing how to massage a young man's ego, he said, "Well, you have learned a lot here." That did it. I doubtless communicated with my parents, but the *beau geste* was to resign both fellowships I had gained, to make space for an alternate. For I had a clear sense that this step had to be now or never, for no telling whom I might meet in Europe! I did have to tell Helen Malits, though, who was then a year behind me at Saint Mary's College, whom I intended to invite to our celebratory weekend (the "senior prom"). As if to confirm the image of a callous young man, I invited her to the weekend, only to announce that I would be "entering the seminary" in the fall. We did manage to have fun that weekend, however, and our lives together would later open up in unexpected ways, though nothing could then have predicted that. We would have to say goodbye at graduation, though it was not until later, driving home to Akron with my parents, that I broke down with my sister, feeling that she could appreciate that sort of loss, also needing her help to feel how Helen must have felt.

I thought of myself as having a number of good friends, most of whom took the news about my intent to "enter Holy Cross" about as well as young men fretting about their own next step possibly could. The most difficult to tell was Peter Stavis. Peter had been with us from the outset, and I found him the most interesting, indeed exotic, of our remarkable initial class in the program. The only child of a Greek father and (as we thought) an English mother, Peter came from Fond du Lac, Wisconsin, where he had become Catholic in high school. (While we had done a lot of things in high school, becoming Catholic had not been one of them!) Moreover, he was also an artist who tried his hand at painting icons, soon discovering that Catholics did not have to be "Roman" but could be "Greek," or Melkite. By this time, in our senior year, Peter had given up on dorm life and was living with Waldemar Gurian's widow, Edith (or "Mama") Gurian, a remarkably cultured émigré from Germany whose husband had been Notre Dame's most distinguished international relations professor. They had barely escaped the Gestapo in the thirties, later to find refuge at Notre Dame with a number of other émigrés, mostly Jewish, as were Edith and Waldemar, though both had become Catholics in university. So Peter introduced me into a number of worlds, and I reciprocated by inviting him to my brother Paul's wedding over Thanksgiving of our final year, wanting him to experience a family fest. My parents loved him, and he would later show them Athens after my ordination to priesthood in Rome. So our friendship would blossom, but at that moment, I knew his reaction to my news would be negative, nor was I disappointed, so we agreed to separate for now, never realizing what the future would hold.

Four delightful years of college life culminated in a delightful western drive with my sister to San Francisco to meet her fiancé, where we joined our parents, who had come by train. We all took advantage of a newspaper publishers' meeting at the Del Coronado outside San Diego, California, followed by a drive north on the celebrated State Route 1, touring the Hearst mansion in San Simeon and hearing inside stories about the life there from an American Field Service friend of my father, the advertising director of the *San Francisco Chronicle*, a Hearst newspaper. Then we traveled north to Montana, revisiting my father's family haunts, and across the Dakotas to Minnesota for a brief stop at Jordan, where I would be entering our Holy Cross novitiate in less than a month. A valedictory tour, we bonded as a "second family," as both my sister and I were on the cusp of taking up a new life. Our father's customary thoughtfulness found the meeting as an excuse for us to spend extended time together.

The novitiate year proved to be salutary for me; I had thought—as a General Program graduate—that I would spend the time reading the church fathers. (Louis Putz had counseled that the best reading would be of someone with "St." before his name rather than "STD" after it.) In fact, I spent my time coming to know (and to appreciate, after a fashion) young men mostly four years younger than I, just out of the "little sem" (or high school seminary), with little experience of life. Yet thanks to a remarkable priest, George Schidel, who directed me to reading Hans Urs von Balthasar's *Thérese of Lisieux*, I was able to treasure this year apart, grow a bit in prayer, and come to appreciate Holy Cross at a remove from Notre Dame. Father Bill Evans, whose simple missionary love for East Bengal touched my heart, gave our final retreat, and may well have implanted a desire to serve there. He would give his life for his people in 1971, killed by Pakistani troops during the Bengali struggle for independence, where people still honor his grave.

A year "in vows" at Moreau Seminary at Notre Dame followed, where I was asked to do more philosophy by people who failed to appreciate the depth and tenor of our program, but managed to supplement it with the study of languages (Latin, Greek, and German) as well as tutorials with Arnold Ross, the generous and imaginative chairman of mathematics, who led me into linear algebras. This remarkable intellectual *tour de force* turned out to be excellent training for the mental gymnastics required to follow theology lectures by refined and astute mentors in Latin at the Gregorian University in Rome. I reconnected with YCS students during this interim year, among them Helen Malits, who had spent her junior year in Vienna and traveling Europe. As soon as it was determined that I would be among those headed for Rome, I could hardly wait. For having duly foregone European study to honor the call to Holy Cross, it seemed serendipitous that the opportunity would return in another mode. Yet I must also have appreciated how sheltered our undergraduate experience had been, despite the superior intellectual challenges of the General Program, and the windows on the world that YCS study weeks had afforded. Europe was clearly calling, in the form of our religious community of Holy Cross, assigning me to Rome for study, as well as my own psyche, which relished exploring wider horizons. Once again, my innate propensity to love whatever I engaged in could see only possibility in the prospect of study in Italy—no hesitation, and even less anxiety.

2

Rome

VENTURING INTO HOLY CROSS had been undertaken with a sense of necessity. I needed to respond one way or another to the lingering sense that the Lord was calling me to serve others as a priest, so entering the novitiate year with Holy Cross seemed a prudent way to test that call. Yet I came to realize during that year, and increasingly as time went on, that it was not so much priesthood I was searching for, but a community of faith among brothers and sisters, and I had serendipitously hit upon this one. Attempting to describe these steps will require a great deal of indirection, however, since their rightness can only appear in retrospect. As Jung puts it in the last chapter of his autobiography, we cannot know in advance whether a decision is correct; we can only make it so by being faithful to it. (Yet for other brothers and sisters in Holy Cross, that fidelity would lie in following their individual call out of religious life into marriage, so one literally never knows.) Yet as my own story unfolds, many factors will contribute to a continuing sense of fidelity: key among them the role of Jung refracted through Helen Luke's guidance, as well as the contribution of Ignatius of Loyola, through directed retreats following the pattern of his "Exercises."

But for now, Rome beckoned these young Americans ready to undertake an education in theology to prepare them for priesthood in Holy Cross. A severe culture shock awaits any Anglo-Saxon encountering Italy, which will quickly bring Catholics to realize how Protestant are our sensibilities. I came to feel that enculturation to Italians and things Italian would offer an invaluable preparation for any Westerner intending to serve in Asia or Africa as well. Debarking in Naples, we were met at the door of our house in Rome by our older confreres, announcing an in-house seminar on recent writings of Bernard Lonergan for the next day, asking us to prepare for it by reading the first of five articles on "*Verbum*: Word and Idea in Aquinas." That sudden welcome touched some of us deeply, who came to relish his masterful presentation of the key theological doctrines of incarnation and trinity, and went on to follow his seminar on grace in Thomas Aquinas. It is difficult to describe the effect of this powerful yet inviting intellect on those of us willing to follow his rigorous logical expositions. His mode of teaching always involved exploring, embodying theology as "faith seeking understanding" (Augustine), and so presented a lively contrast to the "need for certitude" that often dominates popular understandings of theology, and too often its academic exposition as well. As I have had to acknowledge, moreover, I am a philosopher, and so found his conceptual rigor as attractive as others may have found it off-putting. It is fair to say that his spirit suffused the four years of study, turning them into a progressive and unceasing inquiry.

Summers in the Südtirol introduced us to the beauty of the Dolomite region of Italy while affording the opportunity to pursue German in conversation with the children who lived around us in Sarns-bei-Brixen. (We would then continue the practice between classes at the Gregorian during the year. The only language I could not learn in an Italian milieu was Spanish, given their proximity; that had to wait for a return to the United States and the presence of lively Mexican sisters in our seminary at Notre Dame.) But the Südtirol afforded more than beauty and a new language. In my case, it provided the occasion for spending a summer in slow meditative reading of Teresa of Avila and especially John of the Cross, whose philosophical acumen attracted me powerfully. I had already selected an American Carmelite for spiritual director in Rome, but what offered this occasion was a mildly frightening series of tension attacks at the end of my second year of theological studies. I say "mildly" because anyone as intensely concentrated on study as I have been should probably know enough to expect something of that sort. We were all invited to prepare study projects for the time in the mountains, yet that spring the doctor not only exempted me from that, but insisted that I not undertake anything of the kind. So I was blessedly diverted into a life-shaping meditative reading of John of the Cross—deliberately not pursued in a "scholarly mode." While that manner of reading could hardly survive continuing academic pursuits, that summer's *lectio divina* would decisively shape my interior life.

One person is regularly designated to be "superior" of a religious house, to oversee good order and be responsible administratively for the spiritual welfare of house members. I say "administratively" because a religious superior is not a "spiritual director" (or guide) so much as one who assures that such guides are made available, and that people avail themselves of them. Needless to say, this is a particularly telling responsibility when the members are "in formation," that is, vowed members in the process of coming to a mutual decision between themselves and the community. Our superior was Edward Heston, CSC, an energetic man in his fifties, trained in canon law and very much at home in Rome. He modeled many things for us, in his fidelity to common prayer with us, as well as his linguistic alacrity, yet our particular group challenged his administrative skills considerably, it seems, since we were reputed to "have ideas of our own," and we did. Yet we also understood our vow of obedience to him as our superior, even if we found ourselves often taking issue with policies and attitudes. Yet he respected our forthrightness, an outstanding virtue of his as well, to be put to the test as press officer of Vatican Council II.

In my own case, our relationship as it developed taught me how to respond to people temperamentally inclined to bully others, as he was. When an occasion arose when I had to challenge him directly on a matter of little consequence, I came to realize that this penchant was not deliberate, so to call him a "bully" would be less a judgment than a factual observation. Noticing that I instantly gained his respect, I came to see that we have no choice but to stand up to bullies—for their sake as well as our own! In any case, he proved to be a good superior for our group, as well as for others following us. I have sketched how salutary was my incident with him. Even when he found himself unable to approve two of our number for continuing studies in Rome, their return to the United States for studies turned out to be the best for each of them, despite (or perhaps) because of the humiliation involved for them. So we can each be served by our inabilities as well as our abilities, as Jesus remarked to Paul in 2 Cor 12:9: "Your weakness leaves room for my power."

At the Gregorian University, the presence of Bernard Lonergan electrified our four years of theology. While other professors proved stimulating, no one came close to Lonergan. Generally speaking, our theological instruction incorporated the sprit of the French *nouvelle théologie*, which prepared us exquisitely for the impending Second Vatican Council. The initial "palace coup," which rejected the preparatory documents of the Roman curia, set up the world's bishops to endorse the basic premise of the French *ressourcement*: that the tradition of the "great church" extended to the beginning, so need not be overdetermined by concerns of sixteenth-century Reformation, to which baroque ("counter-reformation") Catholic theology had succumbed. So we were extraordinarily blessed by our theological formation at the Gregorian. The same could not be said (at that time) for Scripture, despite the fact that the imposing Pontifical Biblical Institute was across the street. So using a house library largely in French, we had recourse to stellar writers on Scripture, notably scholars from the Dominican Ecole Biblique in Jerusalem. Throughout the four years, we learned a great deal from each other in a stimulating international community, with Holy Cross seminarians from North American (including French and English Canada), South America (including Haiti), and South Asia. Friendships from that time continue to animate us, confirming how stimulating theological study can unalterably shape young minds.

I pronounced my final vows in Sarns-bei-Brixen on 16 August 1958, within our gathered community. We were all given ten days and a bit of money to return to Rome in smaller groups each with its own itinerary, so when my parents came to visit later that summer, Father Heston made an exception to permit me to travel with them through Italy, so I could introduce them to some of our favorite places. As we came to Venice, my father suggested that I put a sign in the seminary where he knew my confreres would be staying, inviting them all to supper that evening. So Dad and I went to a trattoria for lunch, where I explained to the proprietor our plans for the evening. "Va bene," he said, showing how he would enlarge the place by moving the potted plants to the edge of the canal. My mother enjoyed being the only woman present, and the mixed seafood with Veneto wine offered an unforgettable evening. One more example of our founder Basil Moreau's attention to family, as our unique mix of men and women, lay and clerical, comes together quite naturally in those familial terms that his original vision had limned.

A year and a half later, my parents returned to celebrate four of us being ordained to the priesthood just before Advent 1959, following the Roman pattern. This would allow us to serve in parishes for Christmas and the remainder of our academic year. The first confession I heard—and the only one I have been free to tell—was of an enterprising man who spotted a young priest sitting out in the open, only to confess, "Padre, ho fatto un po di tutto"—"I have done a little bit of everything!" So since he told nothing, I can relate it as a lovely vignette of Italian Catholic culture! My parents made a point of including my confreres whose parents could not be present. From our stay in Assisi, where we had been before, two things stand out. On the previous visit, I had tried to incorporate modest hostels into our itinerary so that my parents would have some idea of how we normally lived. In Assisi I overdid it, only to hear my mother complain sharply (through the flimsy door connecting our respective rooms): "Roger, this bed is impossible!" His response was typical: "Hell, Nancy, if Saint Francis could do it, so can we! Let's put the mattress on the floor." Another Tuscan episode involved shopping with my mother for shoes in Florence—hardly my favorite pastime. Yet Florentine Italian is so mellifluous that I spent the entire time asking the salesgirl questions, so I could hear her answers, without interrupting the process, for my mother loved the shoes as well! With regard to accommodations in Rome, however, both that time and the next, my father outsmarted me, taking up residence at the Hassler at the Spanish Stairs. When they returned for ordinations, the desk clerk recognized them, asking them if they wanted "their room" back. My father could only admire his acute marketing sense.

At the end of our studies, three of us had to make our way back to Rotterdam for the sea journey home. Our years in Rome had been restricted to travel in Italy itself—a minuscule hardship!—perhaps to offset envy on the part of our brothers who had not enjoyed the privilege of studying in Europe; our gallivanting around Europe could have been divisive of community life. So we managed on our way back to Holland to visit Spain, with the Family Rosary group working with Father Peyton, notably Jerry Lawyer and Joe Quinn, sterling older brothers witnessing an enviable freedom that inspired us. It turned out that Marcos McGrath was in Madrid, enroute to Rome with Cardinal Silva of Santiago, Chile. I was stunned when he asked me to come to the airport with him in the Vatican nuncio's car, only to watch the ubiquitous guards lining the street to the airport (in Franco's time) stand to attention at the Vatican flag, while the airport gates opened onto the tarmac to allow the driver direct access to the plane itself. On the way back, I felt a bit compromised riding in that car, registering it as one more experience of the potential for clerical corruption—a salutary lesson for one newly ordained! The next stop, Lourdes, impressed us all with its simplicity and human presence. The lore is that everyone who comes to Lourdes seeking a cure returns healed, whether they be cured or not! For the power of God can alter our very relationship to all that we have and are, as my confrere John Dunne noted so well in his *Time and Myth*.

Some of us returned to a pastoral year at Notre Dame, especially needed for those who had studied in Rome, where pastoral dimensions were conspicuously absent in an assiduously theological curriculum. We had felt the absence acutely, so some of us organized weekly visits to a clinic for cancer patients, to remind ourselves that we were preparing for service as priests. Even without supervision, it could offer a taste of what our lives were to encounter, as well as a fresh perspective on theology. I shall never forget a man suffering from throat cancer instructing me one day: "The Pope [Pius XII] says that one cannot be Catholic and Communist. What does he know about that? I have been both all my life!" In fact, Lonergan's way of introducing us to theology as "faith seeking understanding" helped me appreciate the wisdom of this remark, as his influence fostered a keen pastoral sense by preparing us to turn nearly any situation into a theological learning experience. So four intercultural and theologically exciting years in Rome set the stage for the further study demanded if I would teach in university as a Holy Cross religious. What I loved best of all, though, was Italy: her food, her mellifluous language, her spontaneous people. And as the name "Italia" is feminine, one can only refer to the country in feminine terms, so what Italy taught me above all was to love.

Rome Perdures

The greatest gift Roman study gave to us in Holy Cross was to be with brothers from the rest of the world: Haiti, Brazil, East Bengal (then East Pakistan), and Canada, notably Quebec and the Maritimes. As brothers one to another, we not only came to appreciate our diverse cultures, but also to learn each other's languages during the rotating years of "house languages." And as Catholics, we came to realize how Roman directives are framed to state an ideal for the rest of the world, yet seldom taken that seriously in Rome. This would prove to be effective inoculation against erstwhile pharisees who regularly appeal to Rome, and immediately prepared us for the revolt of the world's bishops at the outset of Vatican II, who rejected the prepared documents to forge their own: for what licenses Roman curial officials to state an ideal for the rest of the world? Yet the surrounding Italian culture would also inoculate us against cynicism. As my friend David Tracy would remark some years later (1969), when we gathered for a retrospective on Vatican II at Perkins School of Theology in Dallas to find our interlocutors quite uncomfortable, fearing that the council may have trumped the Reformation's *raison d'être*: "The reason I feel relatively comfortable being Catholic is that I never asked when the church started getting corrupt!" He had studied in Rome just after us, and has written eloquently of the way Bernard Lonergan's witness continues to animate our theological inquiry.

Many years later (2002), when those of us who gather annually to celebrate Lonergan's witness migrated from our customary Boston College site for a celebratory week in Rome, we repaired each evening to Santa Maria in Trastevere for prayer with the Communità de San Egidio, a celebrated lay group that had brokered the Mozambique peace accords, stimulated by an indigenous priest who had lived with them in Rome during his studies. Nothing better than chanted evening prayer followed by supper in Alfredo's! At that time I was also able to meet Timothy Radcliffe, OP, on leave from Oxford to serve as Dominican Master. Visiting Santa Sabina on the Aventine hill with a Downside Benedictine, Sebastian Moore, Timothy greeted us with an aperitif on their balcony overlooking Saint Peter's, suggesting that the commanding view might explain why he "had accepted the job!" Dominicans share the coveted Aventine address with Knights of Malta and the Benedictine abbey of San Anselmo, where the Abbot Primate resides. Rembert Weakland (who had previously studied music with my sister-in-law, Rachel Ober, at Julliard) served in that capacity for a number of years, and told me of his connection with the community of San Egidio. Shortly after their foundation as a lay community, realizing the need for theological study, they approached various Roman institutions. Rembert invited them to attend classes at San Anselmo, which specializes in liturgy, then helped their music group to spend a summer at Chevtogne, a monastery in Belgium long linked with Eastern Christianity. There they assimilated the haunting chant that makes their Trastevere evening prayer a haven for believers of many traditions. Later yet, a colloquy at Castel Gandolpho exploring creation *ex nihilo* with Jews, Christians, and Muslims brought me into Rome with the Muslim delegates, and their friend assigned to Italy for Turkish television told us he often prayed in the evening with the San Egidio community.

So Rome remains a destination for me; "mi trovo à casa à Roma"—I feel at home in Rome. Dealings with the Vatican over the years have largely been restricted to the secretariats for Christian Unity and for Interreligious Dialogue. An American Paulist priest, Tom Stransky, later rector at Tantur (where he will be introduced), had helped initiate the Christian Unity secretariat with the Dutch Cardinal Willebrands, at the behest of Paul VI. Michael Fitzgerald, an Irish Missionary of Africa with a British passport, long directed the secretariat for Interreligious Dialogue. These two offices, dedicated to outreach, attracted imaginative staff who offered consistently fresh perspectives on both church and world. Visiting them reminded me of the Rome that had animated our theological study from the outset, providing the "fresh air" that John XIII had promised from Vatican II. Needless to say, the rest of the Vatican lives in another century, as a visit to the Secretariat of State (in 1981) made clear to me. As rector of Tantur Ecumenical Institute in Jerusalem, I needed to report to Christian Unity (to whom we are accountable) as well as to the Secretariat of State, given the situation in Jerusalem. Pièrre Duprey (another Missionary of Africa) was my interlocutor, and after an extended conversation catching up on "the situation" in Israel/Palestine, he reverted to the Italian expression "per dire la verità [to tell the truth]," to which I retorted: "What have we been speaking up to now—Romanità?" Such is the way with Rome, illustrated by John Henry Newman's response (later in his life as cardinal) to friends who asked whether he had been to Rome recently: "My father explained to us children that queasy travelers should never venture too close to the engine room!"

So Rome has ever been profoundly ambiguous for Catholics, as it also was for Martin Luther or Freud. I am told that the bishops assembled for Vatican I had to reject the schemata prepared for them as well. True or not, the revolt inaugurating Vatican II remains paradigmatic. Yet neither curial officials nor those bishops infected with *Romanità*—a supine attitude ready to forego the "ordinary jurisdiction" afforded them by episcopal ordination to curry favor with curial officials—seemed to have learned the lesson that "the church" does not reside in Rome. More than any single message, this was the existential experience of Vatican II, issuing in the idiom of "people of God" as a counterpoint to structural ecclesiastical procedures of governance. As commentaries on Vatican II remind us, its documents ever hold church as structure in tension with church as people of God. Yet in the face of worldwide experience of a people of God flourishing, many countries, with Rome itself, are witnessing the implosion of church as structure. As authorities oblivious of their disconnect from people of God continue to undermine their own authority behind veils of secrecy and a reluctance to take counsel, especially with intelligent women, one can only pray that the Spirit's presence to the church as a whole will indicate to the church as structure ways to reform itself. Ironically enough, though hardly without historical precedent, some current Roman authorities seem determined to dilute the clear deliverances of our most recent ecumenical council, Vatican II.

Yet for all that, Rome remains a destination, as it once gracefully introduced me to the Mediterranean world. And I have never ceased to recommend it to our younger Holy Cross members as a locale for study, for as it attracts students from the entire world, it continues to offer a bracing cosmopolitan and ecumenical perspective to young Americans. Moreover, a vigorous Italian program at the University of Notre Dame, under the direction of Ted Cachey and Christian Moevs, helps our undergraduate students find a similarly vibrant study venue in Rome. Like Jerusalem, Rome is one of those places where one is never surprised to meet friends: they just happen to be here this year rather than next.

3

Higher Studies Leading to Early Years at Notre Dame

WE HAD "RETURNED" TO Notre Dame—a mode of expression common to Holy Cross priests—eager to participate in the program introducing us to ministry, and ready for our next step. If the steps to this point had been taken together, our individual talents would now be given room to shine. I was invited to teach philosophy to a group of extraordinarily bright sophomores, selected by the legendary professor of English, Frank O'Malley, whom Charles Sheedy, CSC, now Dean of the College of Arts and Letters, had asked to tailor an academic program that would challenge our most talented students. The course in question was titled "Philosophy of Man," and the chair of the department had assigned his own book, *Philosophical Psychology*, as the text for all courses. Taking one look at it, I realized I could not endorse it, nor would it wash with these students. Besides, my General Program background had left me with a predilection for original texts. So I worked up a syllabus respectful of the area, constructed from primary texts. I was careful to note, however, that the text for the class was Herman Reith, CSC, *Philosophical Psychology*. On the first day, as we went through the syllabus together, one of the students noticed that there were no assignments listed from the purported text, so they readily concluded there was no text, only original readings. I had to disabuse them of that, of course, so asked them to repeat after me: "The text for this course is . . ."—telling them that the first exam question would be to name the text. They got it, and we went ahead. My confrere was a gentle person, and never raised it as an issue, though I was sure the dean would support me, for he had inaugurated this program precisely to give bright students some relief from a standard curriculum.

Theodore Hesburgh, CSC, as president, had also been waiting to remove the vestiges of a French boarding school by alleviating a number of the draconian rules governing residence life. So I was appointed to a committee of faculty and administrators to do just that. In the process, however, we came up with a fresh approach to residence life, whereby students who had moved from one hall to another as they progressed through four years would be assigned to a single hall for their entire time. Two realities pressed for this: the custom of freshman halls hardly led to proper enculturation, while it also favored a subgroup of rectors fixated on discipline. Moreover, the university was also expanding, and we felt that smaller units would make for greater familiarity, even if they would also restrict the amplitude of one's acquaintances. (The college system I had heard about at Yale was also a factor, though we could never duplicate dining facilities in each hall.) Living, as Holy Cross priests tend to do, in a residence hall with students gave plenty of practice to the counseling and pastoral skills to which we were being introduced.

My intellectual predilection for philosophy was clear enough, so Ernan McMullin, an Irish philosopher of science and a priest whose humane spirit had recently begun to enrich the Notre Dame faculty, recommended that I study at Yale, where he had experienced a stimulating sabbatical year. His astute political sense perceived how valuable graduate study would be for networking, yet Catholic religious communities had customarily sent their members to study philosophy in Europe. Ernan's Yale experience convinced him that graduate study in America would better serve Notre Dame's ambitions, as articulated by President Hesburgh, who had personally invited Ernan to Notre Dame from Louvain a few years before. Yet members of religious congregations must petition for study, to acknowledge the communal dimension of our work, and I feared it would take some persuasion to be permitted to go Yale, given the ingrained predilection for Europe. Had any American Catholic priest ever undertaken philosophical studies at a university like Yale? The answer at that time, interestingly enough, was no. Although the distinguished Jesuit John Courtney Murray had taught there for a semester in the previous decade, the fields of philosophy and theology had a sacred aura about them, so religious congregations could easily find ostensibly secular institutions inappropriate for such study.

Laval in Québec

Fortunately, however, we had forward-looking leaders in Holy Cross, one of whom was serving as Director of Studies for the congregation. While he had earned his doctorate at Laval University in Québec, he proved open to the possibility of Yale or Princeton. He only asked that I immerse myself in textual study of Thomas Aquinas for a year at Laval, before proceeding to further study. What might have been construed as a "test of obedience" seemed quite reasonable to me, and in retrospect proved utterly serendipitous. Imagine a year spent *en français*, focusing on Aquinas' texts with teachers who knew them thoroughly, along with the opportunity to experience yet another culture! And since our religious congregation had developed both in the United States and in Québec, I would come to know my Canadian confreres better as well, spending holidays with them in Montreal. Moreover, a Holy Cross confrere, Tom Feely, was completing his doctoral studies at Laval at the same time, so evening walks together on the promenade of the Château Frontenac cemented a lasting friendship.

At that time (1961–62), the province of Québec was governed by the iron hand of a premier named Duplessis who took his cues from the bishops: Christendom *redivivus*. But the philosophy faculty was still located "on the ramparts" in the shadow of the imposing Château Frontenac, and the students were quite lively. (I was to meet one years later in Ecole Biblique in Jerusalem who reminded me of the good times we had together.) And the constant practice of French helped make it one of my "second first languages," as Alasdair MacIntyre expresses it. Moreover, I gained a crucial pastoral tip from a visit to a dentist, as he complained bitterly of the quality of the preaching in church. As a patient, of course, I was less than able to respond properly, so he was sufficiently annoyed to confront me directly: "You know the trouble with your guys!" I told him I had not been ordained long enough to appreciate that, so he told me: "You never go to church on Sunday!" I heartily agreed, and from that moment, whenever I am free to do so, I "go to church on Sunday" to see how a clerical caste treats lay folk. The results are mixed, of course, but often surprisingly uplifting.

From that vantage point, in the dead of winter, I decided for Yale rather than Princeton, directing my steps towards New Haven. As it turned out, while Yale did not count the year at Laval towards residency, they permitted me to take comprehensive examinations after one year, which I did, so the year counted after all! But yet more telling was the experience of concentrated textual study of Aquinas at Laval, in the wake of the intellectual stimulation afforded by studies with Bernard Lonergan. I was then equipped to move beyond a narrowly "Thomist" construal of Aquinas, setting the stage for appreciating his thought in its proper context with its potential reach. (All of this would eventually bear fruit in a monograph, *Aquinas: God and Action* [1979], later to be extended to include interfaith perspectives, *Knowing the Unknowable God* [1986].) The shift to New Haven, however, involved concentrating on analytic philosophy and logic, necessary tools for doing Anglo-American philosophy.

Yale in New Haven

Yale proved to be a marvelously hospitable environment, with faculty as well as graduate students. From the outset, I lived with our Holy Cross brothers serving Notre Dame High School in West Haven, in the company of John Gerber, a confrere who had come to pursue a doctorate fresh from studying English with F. R. Leavis at Cambridge. It was a welcoming community experience for us both, as observing the exhausting round of high school teaching no doubt motivated us to complete our doctoral studies. While courses and colleagues proved immensely stimulating, the initial year proved to be a serendipitous time for John and me to discover one another. We took up squash together, while sharing a ministry to our Holy Cross brothers as well as helping in the local parish. The pastor was a marvelous man who soon gave John charge of an outstation that was totally Italian, so he could experience what I had in Rome. (They held their parish council meetings in the local Hofbrau, out of intercultural zeal for good beer!) But we began at that time to share our life of faith and ministry in ways that would bear immense fruit later.

The following year, as another confrere joined us in New Haven to study at Yale and reside with the brothers, I was awarded a Kent

Fellowship (of which more later), which allowed me to reside at More House, the Catholic chaplaincy for Yale. I would spend the entire year on my dissertation, spiked by stimulating conversation in our More House community. A vigorous young diocesan priest, Jim Healy, was Catholic chaplain at Yale, with Edward Seigman, a retired Scripture professor from Catholic University, in residence. Jim had invited his former Scripture teacher at Catholic University to reside at More House when Siegman ran afoul of ecclesiastical authorities in Washington. A mild-mannered priest with a dry sense of humor, Ed Siegman became a favorite of Yale undergraduates, who must have seen a grandfather figure in him. We were preoccupied in those days with the issue of contraception, as Paul VI had called for a lay group to advise him on such matters. I was in contact with Sebastian Moore, a Downside Benedictine serving in a Liverpool parish, whose mimeographed reflections of such matter were transmitted by post across the Atlantic. We were anxious to instruct ourselves, primarily to develop a common policy for hearing confessions. Our dinner table was often consumed by the distinctions needed to probe the issues involved, as well as consulting with our married friends. One evening a bright young Portuguese priest was visiting us, one trained in canon and civil law, and at supper he tried to settle the issue by citing two notable American moral theologians, regularly referred to as "Kelly and Ford." After hearing him out, Jim Healy exploded: "But Healy and Burrell say . . ." and the aura of authority so dominant in Catholic moral thinking suddenly imploded. But when the young man tried to parade his ecclesiastical connections, mentioning Cardinal Cicognani, apostolic delegate to the United States, he touched one who had failed to defend Ed Siegman in the ecclesiastical process mounted against him. So in his impish way, Ed said: "You did know he is chaplain for the mafia, did you not?" So we had fun as well. And on the day President Kennedy was assassinated, in the midst of the trauma all Americans experienced, we called the official chaplain of Yale, Bill Coffin, to ask what we should do at More House: "Dammit, have Mass!" Now that's ecumenism!

Understandably enough, I tended to interact with married graduate student colleagues, probably since our respective lives were already "constituted." So Ernan McMullin's prescient perspective on networking was admirably fulfilled; our cohort proved intellectually engaging at all times, and has continued to communicate, as we can count on each other's assistance. His praise of the faculty was equally prescient. Relations between faculty and students at the graduate level was quite informal. We were blessed with teachers who acted more like colleagues, so introducing us genially into the academic world. My own experience may have been even more informal than others, since my previous study and years of formation gave me a bit of an edge, and perhaps greater access. I shall never forget Russ Hanson's query in the midst of comprehensives. When I answered that they seemed to be going quite well, he retorted: "But you get special help." I should have responded that I was glad he recognized that, for his evangelical family background in Kentucky had purportedly turned him into a village atheist. But I was too slow to pick that up, nor had I any indication of atheistic propensities from his classroom demeanor.

Paul Weiss marched us through Hegel's *Phenomenology of Mind*, Dick Bernstein introduced us to Charles Sanders Peirce, for which I shall always be grateful, while Milton Fisk (who was graduated from Notre Dame a few years ahead of me) led us into philosophy of language, Alan Anderson (with Nuel Balnap) into "relevance logics," and Wilfrid Sellars into Oxford-variety linguistic philosophy with a classical twist. So I was blessed to find mentors in the analytic philosophy and logic that I needed to acquire, yet who also respected the classical frame in which I had been formed, further honed in theological study with Lonergan. I asked our Aristotle teacher, Rulon Wells, to direct my dissertation, when doing early comprehensives assured I could begin in the second year, for he was reputed to be the most expeditious director—and he was.

The enlivening environment of More House was serendipitously supplemented by the unexpected gift of spending favorable weekends crewing an L-19 out of Indian Harbor Yacht Club in Old Greenwich. Wallace Bates had been general counsel of Missouri Bell when my sister was in school in Saint Louis, and became good friends with their daughter Libby. He had been moved to counsel for New York Bell, where he was asked before long to chair the Business Roundtable. Yet he loved to sail, needed a son to crew, and I readily obliged, having learned the art in northern Ontario with a childhood friend, David Gries, who will figure later in this narrative. So after presiding at Sunday eucharist in a black parish on Dixwell Avenue with an avidly literate pastor, Peter Garrity, who read Newman daily, and later became archbishop of Newark, I would board the New Haven Railroad for a sumptuous afternoon in Long Island Sound ("Let's point towards the Empire State Building"). I was to learn later that he had counseled the board of New York Telephone to settle a class action suit brought by female employees regarding salary discrimination, having come to the conclusion that "they are right." When some board members wanted his head, he coolly reminded them that he was only fulfilling his mandate to give them the best advice! Where are the general counsels, or for that matter the bishops, of that era today? Those were the times when American bishops were crafting teaching/learning instruments on peace and on the economy, soliciting broad participation. So richly human a context clearly made it possible to concentrate for fifteen months, to complete the first draft of a dissertation to be published ten years later (1973) by Yale University Press as *Analogy and Philosophical Language*.

What proved fascinating, as well as disconcerting, however, were John Gerber's and my contrasting experiences of Yale. While F. R. Leavis' firm ethical views on literature and its uses were congenial to him, John found the historical criticism in vogue at Yale quite desiccating. Yet he plowed ahead, securing the Leavis connection with a proposed dissertation on D. H. Lawrence's poetry with Harold Bloom. But five years later, as we shall see, a sabbatical semester we spent together in Dallas would significantly alter those plans.

With a dissertation virtually completed after two years, I was set to return to Notre Dame, leaving John in New Haven. Rich and fruitful though the years had been, I was anxious to take my place as a teacher, especially since I turned thirty during my last year, which coincided with rapid aging in the sixties! I also felt that study had been unduly prolonged—fourteen years, after all, since beginning college! So I was anxious to get to work. There would be formalities to fulfill for a regular position at Notre Dame, of course. The first was to complete the dissertation. I managed that in the interstices of my initial year of teaching, since the "argument" had been honed during fifteen steady months in New Haven, though I was startled to realize how much time completion would take, with details more annoying than stimulating. Defending the dissertation in June 1965, however, provided a joyous homecoming to New Haven, followed by a secure return to Notre Dame. Subsequent narratives will relate how Yale continued to animate me, since the experience there had confirmed Lonergan's mentorship to launch me into a life of unremitting inquiry, an inquiry that would range over diverse fields and topics. Yet again, the uncanny fact that I could love everything I was studying, and especially sustained comparative inquiry into linguistic uses of analogy (or not) in Plato and Aristotle, Aquinas and Scotus, made the years sail along as expeditiously as an L-19 in the sound—how blessed I am!

Teaching as a Holy Cross Priest at Notre Dame

It is virtually impossible to describe the variety and stimulation in the life of a Holy Cross priest-professor at Notre Dame; indeed, incredible as one tries to articulate the round of a typical day. For the charism inherited from our founder, Basil Anthony Moreau, orients us to living with students, introducing us to diverse modes of teaching day and night. Moreover, that demand gives a healthy pastoral dimension to our individual lives, as well as a distinctive stamp to education at our Holy Cross institutions. (Jesuits seem able to make a transcendental argument that teaching Ugaritic is their pastoral work, but we cannot; we are not called to one particular work, but simply to "serve the church.") Moreover, as a group of us had already proposed the more stable mode of residence that had students spending their entire four years in the same hall, we would soon be solicited to inaugurate the new system.

I was asked to be rector of our second-largest hall, named for a president whom I later came to realize had seriously impeded Note Dame's growth to a *bona fide* university, Andrew Morrissey. Working with two confreres returning from study at Yale and Princeton, respectively, John Gerber and Ernie Bartell, we initiated full student participation in governance, to give substantive shape to the proposed changes. The desires of students, however, were often at odds with what remained of the older regime of residence life. One such came to be referred to as "parietals," or visiting hours for women (largely from neighboring Saint Mary's College, for we were still all male). Several patterns were suggested, yet this time the very person who had insisted on altering the French boarding school regime, the president, Father Hesburgh, importunely stated that "we would have parietals over his dead body." What a challenge! How could we prudently test that? So Morrissey Hall proceeded to test it, introducing them on our own. We were duly summoned to the very Dean of Students with whom I had bargained to let John and Ernie join me in Morrissey, where we proposed "seceding from the University." Partly in jest, of course, yet the response was serious: "Fine, but we will cut off your

water and sewage." Before long, the president did relent, however, allowing us to take one more step into a new era.

At the same time, the Vietnam war was heating up, so living with
students vulnerable to induction helped place us firmly in opposition to
a dubiously just war, and before long we found ourselves at the epicenter
of faculty and student protest. One of the most vocal leaders of the student movement against the war, Lenny Joyce, was a Morrissey resident.
So when we got wind of their plans to torch the ROTC building—a frame
structure that would have made a terrific bonfire—I made an appointment with Lenny at the usual time for meeting with students: 11 p.m.,
after the library closed. Without informing Lenny, I prevailed upon Jack
Stevens, colonel in charge of our Army ROTC program, to be there for
that meeting—at 11 p.m. in mufti! Jack came a little early so we could set
it up; when Lenny came in for our discussion, I introduced him to Jack
Stevens, whom he had met and negotiated with as Colonel Stevens. They
knew and respected one another, so it had a chance of working. Jack told
Lenny he had heard the word on the street—Jack kept his ear close to
the ground—and that he respected what Lenny was doing, but that the
ROTC building was in government property, so torching it could land
him in Leavenworth, which was hardly worth it. That Lenny was able to
take such avuncular advice was to his credit, and Jack reciprocated during
the spring ROTC parade when Lenny's cohort organized a sit-down in
the middle of the parade ground. Colonel Stevens, this time not in mufti
but with rows of ribbons on his chest, stared down some beefy football
players lining the field ready to take on the anti-war protesters, marching
his troops neatly around the protesters to save the day.

Given our student body, however, protest was relatively tame, in part
because we were able to tap into established liturgical forms rather than
have to invent rituals of our own. By the fall of 1969, on the day calling
for a national moratorium on the war, John Gerber and I had mounted
a "protest Mass" on the mall facing the impressive new library building.
We had met with our colleagues in the law school to help a dozen students discern the consequences of their resolve to publicly tear up their
draft cards at the "offertory" of that liturgical event. We had found an
anti-war bishop from India to preside, as some of us concelebrated. The
entire congregation then marched the length of our east-west quadrangle,
past crosses with names of solders fallen in Vietnam. We had managed a
dignified liturgical expression of our resistance to a war that increasing

numbers of Americans found to violate just-war criteria. We adults were heartened that a few had decided to withdraw as a result of the careful delineation of penalties and consequences. The FBI was present, photographing us and these students in particular, as the mall was filled with students and faculty, with our president, Theodore Hesburgh, participating from the side.

I was most impressed with the tolerance of our local Holy Cross religious congregation, many of whom had not yet arrived at our conclusions regarding our presence in Vietnam, yet accepted John and me (with others as well) as brothers in a common effort. The spring following, President Hesburgh came out against the war publicly, in the wake of the death of students at Kent State University. This time classes were suspended, and faculty expressly invited to join those of us living in residence halls, to carry on sustained discussion of the realities involved in protesting US involvement in the war. It was a massive teaching moment, led by our administrators in ways that we found heartening. In fact, I am stupefied by the retrospective spin on the sixties that focuses on drugs and sex, when our experience had been of passionate argument, where "argument" could best be parsed as philosophers are wont to: discussion that substitutes for violence. After all, Catholic social teaching has to have some consequences, does it not? It had failed to stand up to the clear violation of Allied carpet bombing in World War II, and more recently has been effectively sidelined in official Catholic rhetoric by a single issue, abortion.

So each age has specific challenges for a university that intends to be Catholic, but rather than be diverted by ideological sparring, it is worth recalling these events to highlight a day's work with students at Notre Dame. Even when the surrounding world was less troubled, we were ever "on call," spending the wee hours of the morning debating issues of faith with bright young men, or easing them through relationships that can so easily become tangled, as well as negotiating conflicts with parents—to say nothing of unscrambling kinks in their attempt to learn new disciplines. We would come to know their families as well. In my second year teaching, living with Jim Buckley, a stellar confrere and ethicist as we tested "stay hall" in Farley Hall, I came to know Hugh and Mary Fitzgerald through their eldest son, Michael. As a Mount Holyoke graduate, Mary was primary educator in the family, while Hugh, a partner in Coudert Brothers in New York, worked tirelessly for peace, ever displaying a firm yet gentle faith. En route to meetings in the east, my friend Elena and I would visit them at their summer retreat in the Catskills, Elka Park. Their family exhibited a solidarity in trials that might have sunk others. Benedict describes a monastery as "a school of the Lord's service." Living with students proved to be another school forming me as lover; nothing so challenging or rewarding as a pastoral ministry in the midst of young people growing into their potential. It is hardly surprising that so many of us have been invited to witness weddings of former students. The bonding is subtle yet profound, daily yet enduring. And every now and then a student—usually a young woman—would write to express her gratitude. Yet we can hardly live for that, as parents know so well!

4
_____

Chairing Theology at Notre Dame with Alternate Academic Sites: Hyde Park, Bangladesh, Princeton

TEACHING AND SCHOLARSHIP WENT on, of course, in the midst of all this, yet I was blessed by a year's sabbatical that Ernan McMullin, as chair of philosophy, worked to obtained for all junior faculty. An inspired choice sent me only ninety miles west, to Chicago, where I lived in Saint Ambrose, a black parish at the northern edge of Hyde Park, while coming to know Paul Ricoeur, David Tracy, Bernard McGinn, and others at Chicago Divinity School, who would remain lifelong friends and colleagues. A seminar with Paul Ricoeur on "Hegel and Nietzsche" not only enhanced my appreciation of both, but afforded an opportunity to come to know him personally, as we would move to French for coffee after class, to offer him some respite during his first term teaching in English.

Both Hyde Park venues were exciting. From the parish, which extended into North Kenwood, I came to realize the lines were not racial but credit boundaries, while a zealous parish staff and people's vibrant concern for their children's education was inspiring. Hyde Park became an intellectual mecca for me, henceforth easily accessible from South Bend, so the year not only helped me revise my dissertation for publication with Yale University Press, but extended the range of fruitful networking to Chicago. Those were the "Cody years," which made a dedicated Chicago clergy that much more cohesive by effectively depriving them of any leadership. The way that undeniable fact energized rather than demoralized them says a great deal about the potential of post-Vatican II Catholicism for genuine congregational life. I had known some of the leaders from days in Rome, and took part in their meetings to catch the vibrancy of this group, which reminded me a great deal of a religious community. The history of the church in Chicago had been remarkably participatory—often the polar opposite of the East Coast—and that showed in their response to the recent council as well as the current default in leadership.

I had already mortgaged the second semester of 1968–69 to be resident scholar in Perkins School of Theology at Southern Methodist University in Dallas, ostensibly to appropriate the work of Schubert Ogden in "process theology," but as it turned out, more to provide a haven for my friend John Gerber to try to complete his Yale dissertation. That did not happen, but he did betake himself to Alcoholic Anonymous while we were together, which proved a lifelong blessing for him and for countless others whom he served—"we propose; God disposes." We continued to walk with each other until his life was cut short by cancer in 1995 at sixty-four years old, yet his influence on our religious community in that short time would prove incalculable. John helped me realize that dissertations may not be the most significant part of one's life, but friendship clearly is. Perkins School of Theology offered a welcome venue, particularly in the person of Albert Outler, an articulate student of John Wesley and one of the great ecumenists in the spirit of Vatican II, where he had served as an observer. Schubert Ogden and I agreed to disagree, sometimes vehemently, yet that experience presciently prepared me for ecumenical exchange in the role of theology chair at Notre Dame. As further experience in theological education would show, my real objection turned on his sequestering medieval inquiry into an ideological cul-de-sac called "classical theism," which purportedly offered justification for the vagaries of Christendom. I bristled at the way this purportedly "critical" assessment twisted medieval inquiry to fit a procrustean modernist template, quite uncritically presuming Enlightenment categories to be normative. Moreover, that specific ideology would betray theological students by offering them an excuse to remain ignorant of the rich medieval archive of theology. Nothing like that would ever have occurred to historical scholars like Al Outler, however, so the Perkins milieu helped me appreciate the decisively critical role that history must play in theology, preparing me for the robust colleagueship of Robert Wilken, one of the first of whom I was able to engage in our faculty at Notre Dame.

Chairing Theology at Notre Dame

The two sabbatical venues of Chicago Divinity School and Perkins School of Theology had helped direct my training in logic and Anglo-American philosophy towards issues of philosophical theology, so it seemed natural to accept the university's request to chair the department of theology in the spring of 1970. Those who appointed me—notably my predecessor, James Tunstead Burtchaell, CSC, newly appointed provost—challenged us to develop a faculty of theology engaged in ecumenical inquiry in a Catholic university. So the next decade proved the most intellectually stimulating to date, as I came to realize how theological inquiry can bring philosophical issues to a fine point, with superb colleagues assisting us to fulfill the mandate. Serendipitously, my tenure as chair dovetailed with Father Hesburgh's launching the Tantur Ecumenical Institute in Jerusalem, while departmental tasks included incorporating a Judaica position into our faculty, offered to the university by the Bronfman family in honor of Father Hesburgh. Joseph Blenkinsopp, Stanley Hauerwas, Robert Wilken, and John Howard Yoder suggested we do that by reconfiguring Hebrew Scriptures, New Testament, and early church under the rubric of Judaism and Christianity in Antiquity. Ironically, if ours had been a faculty of religious studies, we could easily have engaged someone to teach rabbinics without altering anything at all. As it was, however, we learned how to welcome a Jewish colleague into the very heart of the study of theology as we saw it. This collegial development showed me that administration can expand disciplinary horizons, and would soon direct me to explore the fruitful interaction among Jewish, Christian, and Muslim intellectuals in medieval times, a step that would engage both Jerusalem and Cairo.

Our shared perspective on theology, responsive to the *ressourcement* of Vatican II, was expressly ecumenical. We viewed theological inquiry as spanning the entire Christian tradition, intent on retrieving what we could learn from it. We were engaged in the seventies in joint projects with Valparaiso University (Lutheran), the Divinity School at the University of Chicago, Yale Divinity School, and Union Theological Seminary. Yet interacting with those institutions, which trained most of America's teachers in religious studies or theology, would also teach me how Catholic our perspectives were. For at Notre Dame we considered the Christian tradition as a seamless garment, while they did not. Their curriculum divided the "study of theology" (purportedly begun with Schleiermacher in the nineteenth century) from the "history of Christian thought," which was meant to expound the entire tradition as "background" to a critical study of theology. This ideological divide was shaped by a Reformation mentality as well as Hegel's bifurcation of inquiry into "premodern" and "modern," where "modern" alone was deemed to be "critical." Serendipitously, however, the presence of formidable teachers at these key institutions subverted this ideology to help students appreciate the theological merit of patristic and medieval thinkers—notably, Jaroslav Pelikan at Chicago, Robert Calhoun at Yale, and Cyril Richardson at Union. These spiritual and intellectual leaders provided us with interlocutors who could fertilize our efforts as we could theirs for a critical as well as ecumenical retrieval of a rich tradition. In short, the polar opposite of the "process theology" project, which seems hardly to have outlived Schubert Ogden's academic career. So much for episodes in "systematic theology" bereft of historical and hermeneutic resources.

Our academic location was rather unusual among our peer institutions, for we were a department of theology in a university, which meant that we educated both graduates and undergraduates. In fact, we taught a quarter of the student body each year, for all students—regardless of their course of study—were required to take two courses in theology. We continually pondered how that selection should be organized, settling on a first course combining Hebrew Scriptures and New Testament with the first five formative centuries of the church. Ambitious, certainly, though not meant to be comprehensive so much as lead to literacy in the subject. The second course was open to treat a significant topic of Christian theology in whatever way appeared best to the teacher. (I long taught a course in psychology and religion, for example, which culminated with Sebastian Moore's *The Crucified Jesus Is No Stranger*, to show students how classical psychological perspectives can enrich the ways we reflect on religious issues.) Adding a graduate program to this list of responsibilities may sound like a lot, but on assuming the office we were also presented with an MDiv program preparing students for ministry. Many of our peer institutions were divinity schools, more or less integrated into the university of which they were a part, but without an undergraduate component. It continued to be our conviction that the possibility of teaching all levels of students enhanced our faculty's perspectives on the discipline. Moreover, the MDiv program took us into the rich field of "theological education" as most divinity schools understood it. To be sure, combining professional education with a conventional graduate program stretched us as well, but it reflected the mixed character of theology as Aquinas has elaborated it: a discipline as practical as it is speculative.

As chair, I sought to accommodate our faculty who needed the extra income of teaching summer school while dedicating my own summers to scholarship. The presence of a superb administrative assistant, Anne Fearing, allowed me to absent myself to find venues for uninterrupted writing: one summer in the university's Land O' Lakes retreat in Wisconsin, another at the University of Portland, a third at our Holy Cross novitiate in Bennington, Vermont. A dear friend, Agnes Crone, had warned me early on: protect your summers! A Sister of Charity of Nazareth, Kentucky, Aggie had assisted us in a 1968 Carnegie summer institute in "Philosophy of Religion," promoted by Ernan McMullin, for teachers in Catholic colleges in need of research time and a decent library. Given our extensive involvement with students at all levels during the year, her advice proved prescient. Not only did I need to model what we expected of others; I realized how much I needed this time and space for scholarship as well. Thanks to this resolve in the midst of administration, writing became an indispensable spiritual discipline.

I had already recast my Yale dissertation on "analogy and philosophical language" into a book while on sabbatical in Hyde Park (published, thanks to Jaroslav Pelikan, by Yale University Press in 1973), and nine years of administration would yield two further studies, each calling upon philosophical skills cognate to our goals as a theology faculty: *Exercises in Religious Understanding* (1974) and *Aquinas: God and Action* (1979). I was also privileged to serve under two stellar deans: Fred Crosson, whom we shall meet later as teacher and scholar, and Isabel Charles, a fair-minded pioneer among women administrators in our predominantly male environment. I had to confess to her that whenever I returned to my office and received a callback message from "Dean Charles," the little boy in me queried: "What have I done wrong now?" Gender pervades our lives, as we shall narrate later.

Yet chairing such a large department, and one so critical to the university's mission, perforce engaged me in wider university concerns: academic council, faculty senate, as well as numerous ad-hoc committees to address specific issues. My greatest achievement in academic council was to shepherd through a proposal for regular part-time faculty, triggered by our desire to engage a husband-wife couple to guide field education in our MDiv program. "Regular part-time" was specifically designed to enable spouses to split a faculty position, if they so desired, yet enjoy fringe benefits denied to adjunct faculty. To be sure, it especially envisaged women who may not want to try to do everything normally asked of full-time faculty, given their familial responsibilities. The proposal was properly scrutinized in the academic council, as it should have been, but the myopia of science and engineering faculty was evident in their insistence that "part-time" could hardly be serious. We appeared to be at loggerheads until the first student member of the council, a young woman in engineering, turned to address not the issue but the house (and it was an all-male assembly): "Gentlemen, I do not know whether you are satisfied with your domestic arrangements"—I nearly choked on that one—"but this proposal is designed precisely to allow us to do what you are training us to do, and to do it in the context of family." I had not had the foresight to plan it with her; she spoke from the heart and from her training to date, exhibiting a Catholic sense of family. Her intervention won the day, notably impressing me with the way men are instinctively inclined towards issues while women can more readily address the assembly itself.

The ecumenical task of building an exciting faculty of theology, with the rich human interactions that demanded, required sustained colleagueship, yet our enthusiasm was not shared by all. Some in the university, with some of our colleagues, were quite concerned that the group of faculty whom I clearly counted upon, exhibited by their role in helping us incorporate the Judaica position into our curriculum, were not all Catholic. I had recognized how utterly consonant the sensibilities of Stanley Hauerwas, Robert Wilken, and John Howard Yoder were with what we were doing, so in that sense, how deeply catholic they were. But our more "grammatical" sense of "Catholic" began to give way to a "denominational" sense of the term, as the halcyon days of ecumenism inaugurated by Vatican II were soon to encounter the boundaries inevitably forged by what Lonergan had regularly derided as a "need for certitude."

Moreover, I was quite exhausted after eight years of administration, so a prescient suggestion by my friend John Gerber led to a thirty-day directed retreat in the summer of 1979, one year before completing a third and final term as chair of theology. Discovering the Jesuit retreat house, Eastern Point, on Cape Anne north of Boston, I was blessed with a fine director for the Exercises of St. Ignatius, which led me, some twenty years after ordination to the priesthood in Holy Cross, to a complementary sense of freedom and security in my spiritual and intellectual life. We focused on the Gospel of John, and I shall never forget a meditation towards the end on John 15:15: "I call you not servants, but friends." I realized how I had been "working for him" for a quarter century while he wanted me to be his friend! Everything changed, as the rest of my life would become more explicitly oriented to friendship, while the subsequent year—my last as administrator at Notre Dame—proved quite effortless. I had learned how to "renounce the fruits of my actions," leaving them to the Lord, even to the selection of my successor. Creative displacement to a promontory with nothing between us and the west coast of Ireland had freed the Spirit to do her work.

Fortunately so, for my successor did in fact view "Catholic" in a denominational sense, so before long we would lose two of our key faculty, Stanley Hauerwas and Robert Wilken. By then, however, I was ensconced in the Middle East in an entirely new venue at the Tantur Ecumenical Institute in Jerusalem, while their individual moves turned out to be advantageous for both. Stanley (who has completed his own memoir, *Hannah's Child*, offering his perspective on this transition) would flourish at Duke Divinity School as the stellar Christian ethicist he was meant to be, while Robert worked assiduously to exemplify theological inquiry in a religious studies faculty at University of Virginia, finding his way before long into the Catholic Church. In January 1984, he asked to have lunch with me while I was on retreat outside Charlottesville at a Trappistine house. Immediately upon entering the pub, he asked whether I could find any reason why he should not to become Catholic. Inspired, I said: "Robert, I could find a thousand reasons not to become Catholic, but none against you becoming Catholic!" Stanley would be present as we received Robert into the church at the Dominican House of Studies in Washington in 1994, while the roster of Stanley's students who have become Catholic is considerable. So while the endless round of meetings needed to cultivate our distinctive vision of "doing theology in a Catholic university" would soon become a thing of the past, friendships forged in the midst of such demanding work perdure, and a new life beckoned me forward.

Bangladesh

A prescient shift to include Islam in my intellectual and emotional perspectives had been presaged in 1975, in response to an invitation from
our farseeing Holy Cross provincial superior, Bill Lewers, to teach for a
semester in Bangladesh. So in the wake of a Jewish-Christian-Muslim
summer colloquy at Tantur, I came to experience a Muslim culture (and
one that is not Arab) in the company of sterling men and women of our
religious congregation serving in East Bengal. My eyes were opened as
my heart could feel a palpable sense of the presence of God that became
the earmark of Islam for me. The delta of East Bengal exudes a quiet
beauty that not even the constant press of people in metropolitan areas
can obscure. Framed by three rivers, with a land mass never much el-
evated above the waters surrounding it, Bangladesh is prey to flooding
and to tropical typhoons, which the Bay of Bengal regularly generates.
Moreover, Bangladeshis are extraordinarily handsome, with fine features
and a gentle composure, while the sari is easily the most flattering female
dress, as it can be beautifully modest.

The Holy Cross religious community of men and women is now
overwhelmingly Bangladeshi, with most ethnically Bengali, but we work
with an increasing number of people more oriental in mien, who live on
the periphery of the land of the Bengalis (Bangladesh). So, feeling mar-
ginalized by the Muslim majority, they have been quite open to Christian
evangelization. A poor country, Bangladesh has become increasingly
self-sufficient in food while its political volatility seems as endemic as the
corruption it generates. Yet its people celebrate with song, flowers, and
dance; in fact, nowhere have I found young men so adept at floral arrangements. Their skill as chefs, moreover, is legendary, affording steady
work to many itinerant men. Finally, their Islam is best described as "soft,"
with origins in Sufis from Persia.

This privileged an experience in so poor a country called for a response, so I developed a philosophy course on "Issues in Justice," which
proved an exciting way to engage students in assessing their own posture
towards a world that Americans often dominate to the detriment of other
cultures. I was to return to Bangladesh twice more, after having retooled
into Islam, now able to introduce Catholic seminarians into a comparative study of Islam. Not easy, since Christians form a tiny minority—one
half of one percent—so Muslims tend to win every court case. I tried to

help them see that if the statistics were reverse, Christians would invariably win, so it was not a religious issue so much as a sociological one. They were astounded to hear that my American students had seldom even met a Muslim, but understood better when I asked when they had last met a Jew.

The most heartening part of assignments to teach in South Asia, however, was meeting our Holy Cross men and women who had long served there as missionaries, along with our Bangladeshi priests, brothers, and sisters. On mission in Asia, I discovered our founder's vision of Holy Cross as a microcosm of church—male and female, lay and clerical. We work more closely together there, less encumbered by large institutions. I had the same feeling each time I traveled by train through South India, meeting our Holy Cross young men there as well, in a vibrant culture, unforgettable and haunting.

Notre Dame after Jerusalem: 1982–1998

My first year in Jerusalem culminated ten years of administration, as I served as rector of the Tantur Ecumenical Institute for one year. That year (1980–81) and the next one (1981–82) are detailed in chapter 5, devoted to Jerusalem and Cairo, together with all that followed upon that personal and intellectual sea change. The new shape my life took, however, would find fresh expression at Notre Dame until gaining emeritus status in 2006. Engagement with Arabic, culminating in translating al-Ghazali, began in Jerusalem and continued though the eighties. These efforts led to a study of the effects of Jewish and Islamic thinkers on Thomas Aquinas' composition of his *Summa Theologiae*. The results of that study detail how this recognizably premier synthesis of Christian theology could in fact count as an interfaith, intercultural achievement (*Knowing the Unknowable God* [1986]). Yet before taking up residence in Jerusalem and in Cairo, I had had no inkling of this dimension of Aquinas in my 1979 *Aquinas: God and Action*, so two years in Jerusalem effectively altered my orientation to a world shared by Jews, Christians, and Muslims.

I began to discuss what I was learning with students in America, largely at Notre Dame, but also at Princeton Theological Seminary (1986) and later at Hartford Seminary and Hartford University (1998). Two more teaching stints at the National Major Seminary in Dhaka also enhanced my understanding of a non-Arab Islam. Participation in the first Mulla Sadra conference in Tehran in 1999 opened up the Shi'ite intellectual world in the person of this seventeenth-century philosophical theologian who wrote in Arabic—Arabic being the Latin of the classical Islamic world. On reflection, while I said that nine years of chairing theology had "proved the most intellectually stimulating to date," the two decades following my retooling into Islamics proved even more stimulating and fruitful.

During this period, summers offered time and space to pursue this new mode of study, assisted by appointment to the Theodore Hesburgh chair in the College of Arts and Letters—an interdisciplinary chair offered me in 1988 on returning from Bangladesh. The chair included funds that expedited travel to study venues, notably to the Dominican Institute of Oriental Studies in Cairo, as chapter 5 will detail. Meanwhile, focusing on Jewish-Christian-Muslim exchange in a medieval context catapulted me into the world of today, especially after the two years at Tantur in Jerusalem, so I embraced Raimo Varynen's offer to join the Kroc Institute for International Peace Studies as a faculty Fellow. In fact, while continuing to serve philosophy and theology in a joint appointment, my home increasingly became the Kroc Institute, especially from 1997 when I was asked to assume the direction of our Jerusalem program for undergraduates, requiring residence at Tantur each spring for a period of five years. The effects of that mission will emerge in chapter 5, but it clearly led to a gradual detachment from concerns at Notre Dame, with one foot in the Mediterranean for my final seven years as a regular faculty member, from 1999 to 2006.

Colleagues have always been an integral part of our life at Notre Dame, perhaps the more so since the surroundings of South Bend offer few distractions. It would be impolitic to try to list everyone who has helped shape my intellectual perspectives among our faculty, yet two stand out from the beginning: Fred Crosson and Ken Sayre. Indeed, we collaborated in the sixties on a National Science Foundation project Ken expedited, exploring claims for "artificial intelligence" by way of that generation of computers, programming with cards! Before long, Plato captured Ken's fascination, as his publication record displays, notwithstanding exploring ecological concerns via his "Philosophic Institute." Fred Crosson had initiated me into political philosophy in the General Program as an undergraduate, and became an abiding interlocutor in philosophical inquiry before selflessly serving us as dean, only to continue as an exemplary seminar leader in the Program of Liberal Studies. Our cohort in philosophy included Neil Delaney, David Solomon, Michael Loux, and others, as we accompanied one another from the sixties. Key to our intellectual development was a discussion group meeting monthly, initially focused on the writings of Wittgenstein—a unique learning experience bonding us all. I have already spoken of close companions in our venture in theology. More recently, Cyril O'Regan and Kevin Hart (who soon migrated to Virginia) expanded our horizons appreciably, but I wish to focus on two persons in particular: Gretchen Reydams-Schils and Christian Moevs.

Gretchen Schils and Luc Reydams, from the Flemish community in Belgium, came to Notre Dame with a family of three children: Hendrik and his twin sisters, Elena and Mirjam. Gretchen was appointed to teach ancient philosophy in the Program of Liberal Studies, while Luc, a lawyer, enrolled in our LLM program for human civil rights law. An internship in that program would before long allow them to take the entire family to Tanzania for an internship with the International Criminal Court while Gretchen taught philosophy in a seminary in Arusha. A stint in Congo with her father as a young girl had put Africa in her bloodstream. Gretchen had served as an intern in the European Union after completing initial studies at Leuven, but her aspirations to doctoral studies had been blocked by professors quite unaccustomed to having their authority challenged. A series of serendipitous events, however, gave her the opportunity to study classics at the University of Cincinnati and complete doctoral studies at Berkeley. They imported a European sense of family as well as a Catholic sense of frugality to Notre Dame, going without an automobile for many years through northern Indiana winters.

Gretchen's encounters with a serenely unconscious male hegemony, embedded in a clerical culture, taught me how difficult Catholic academe can be for women. She found her way through these obstacles to tenure, excelling in obtaining fellowships for study in her field of Stoic philosophy, which doubtless commended her to serve as assistant dean for research, and moving on to chair the Program of Liberal Studies. Yet it remains unclear when Notre Dame will become able to tolerate women like Gretchen. A salutary lesson for this cleric! Yet even South Bend, Indiana, can reveal hidden gifts: a talented (and lucky) choreographer helped their twins excel in ballet. Luc's expertise has made him attractive to Leuven's faculty of law, as well as United Nations peacekeeping efforts.

Christian Moevs studied philosophy at Harvard, where his father was a composer on the university faculty of music, yet upon graduation he eluded the academic treadmill by following his mother's path of origins to Italy, and soon after to India, where he submitted to discipline long enough to risk undertaking graduate studies without fear of losing his soul! He elected to study Dante at Columbia with Teodolinda Barolini, emerging at the very moment Notre Dame decided to mount a full-scale program of Dante studies by capitalizing on its long-standing Dante collection (gleaned a century earlier by John Zahm, CSC, whom we shall meet later). When Christian saw the solicitation for a faculty appointment, he said to himself, "That is my job!" and Professor Barolini cooperated with stellar praise. So Notre Dame gained Christian as a colleague in the Romance language faculty. He and I moved quickly to team teaching a course in Aquinas and Dante under the aegis of the interdisciplinary Medieval Institute. That joint effort led him to mine primary philosophy sources to thoroughly recast his original dissertation into *The Metaphysics of Dante's Comedy* (2005), winning the MLA's Marraro Prize as well as the American Association for Italian Studies prize for the best book of 2005. Our friendship has flourished despite intervening distance, as his presence was rewarded by the coveted Sheedy Award for outstanding teaching in the College of Arts and Letters, and he began to share a life with Luke Miller, a Mennonite from Goshen, Indiana, currently engaged in medicine in Chicago, where they now live. Notre Dame can indeed foster unusual and lasting friendships.

The two decades since my initial return from Jerusalem proved quite fruitful, resulting in a study of the vexing issue of freedom in Islamic thought (*Freedom and Creation in Three Traditions* [1993]); a comparative "creation theology" (with Elena Malits, CSC) in *Original Peace: Restoring God's Creation* (1997); a collection of essays articulating what intellectual inquiry has come to mean to me, in *Friendship and Ways to Truth* (2000); as well as two translations of al-Ghazali from Arabic: *Al-Ghazali on the Ninety-Nine Beautiful Names of God*, with Nazih Daher, my Arabic teacher at Notre Dame (1992), and *Al-Ghazali on Faith in Divine Unity and Trust in Divine Providence*—a translation of book 35 of *Ihya' Ulum ad-Din* (2000). A translation project from French with Mary Louise Gude, CSC, and Gerald Schlabach, issued in Roger Arnaldez: *Three Messengers for One God* (1998). Chapter 5 will delineate particulars attending each of these works, for they emerged from a series of intellectual transformations that serendipitously converged, so deserve a properly contextual account. My most nourishing context during this period at Notre Dame, however, proved to be other than academic.

University Village Chaplaincy (1982-1998)

In the years following my initial return from Jerusalem, heart and soul were nourished by a characteristic Holy Cross involvement: chaplain to family student housing at University Village. Recall how the charism inherited from our founder, Basil Anthony Moreau, orients us to living with students, introducing us to diverse modes of teaching day and night. I had resided in men's residence halls for my first sixteen years at Notre Dame, two of them as rector in Morrissey (1966-68). Yet on returning from Jerusalem in 1982, I was called to a small house on the periphery of campus, to serve a community of 132 households, 150 children, and twenty-seven nationalities—mostly graduate students with families.

University Village is a thoroughly interfaith community, with a vibrant Catholic worship group that convened for Sunday Eucharist in the other half of my little house, which served for fifteen years as our community center. So when we eventually cajoled the university into building us a proper center in 1995, we knew what was needed. The telling feature of our community was "the playground," which was surrounded, Conestoga wagon style, by apartment buildings to make a secure open space, with access and egress through the buildings. Since children were the center of our life, the playground epitomized what we were about. Northern Indiana is hardly receptive to outdoor play in winter months, however, so when architects came to consult with us on a new building, we reminded them that the community center should serve for the winter the way the playground does for the summer. So we placed children in the center under a skylight, with a large multipurpose room to one side, surrounded by gathering spaces for food and conversation. Our Sunday Catholic liturgy transforms the multipurpose room, whose potential liturgical use the architects had signaled with a sturdy lintel (replacing a fanciful but totally impractical fireplace) with three small, suggestive stained-glass windows above it. Children have their space and adults theirs, yet all are able to keep eye contact, since the children's space has glass walls. Ministry is seldom about achievements, yet the new community center counts as our greatest, since I came to realize how family student housing regularly ends the list of institutional priorities, with Notre Dame being no exception. I had had to lobby for many amenities, including health care, access roads, and finally this center.

The facility was consistently in use for diverse gatherings. But we found a window of opportunity from noon to three on Sundays, to offer the facility to the Michiana Muslim Community for worship and Qur'an class. A Pakistani couple initiated the venture, which we supported in the village. The husband, Rashid, was later killed in an auto crash on their return to Karachi, so I visited the young widow, Shireen, on my way to Bangladesh in 1994. She met me at the door of her mother's home in Islamabad, asking if I had heard about the miracle. I had, but wanted her version: "We were going for a picnic in Hyderabad [in Sind province] and Rashid asked if we should not pick up an older man waiting for the bus, for it was raining. I cautioned about communal violence, which he discounted for the moment in that region. So we picked him up and I moved to the back seat with the children. Twenty minutes later we had a blowout, and both people in the front seat were killed. If we had not picked up that man, the children would have no parents!"

Once again, we learn from Muslims a palpable sense of the presence of God! Those were the kinds of relationships we enjoyed and fostered, living with young families, with many having their first children thousands of miles from home, and everyone subsisting on graduate student stipends, so that our village fit the poverty roster. I was blessed to have a young woman as assistant, usually the spouse of a student, one of whom had social work training, so identified all the programs for which the income level of our residents made them eligible.

This challenging and nourishing opportunity for ministry sustained me throughout these years of equally dramatic academic transition, by directing my heart to the needs of international student families as I directed the university's attention to their needs. The two sides of my life invariably interacted, as one story will relate. A Muslim family from Cairo connected me with their family when I went there to study one summer, so I was able to share an *iftar* meal at the end of a day in Ramadan. When I returned with gifts for the grandchildren, the student met me, asking if I had met the Saudi couple, for they were "the richest family in the village." (That would not take much, as we have seen.) So the next week, as I made the acquaintance of our new residents, I introduced myself to the Saudi man in Arabic, and he responded that he was "a poor Bedouin from Saudi." Therein lies the story of the Middle East: knowing that I knew the Egyptian, whose riches lie in culture, the Saudi had to eat humble pie; whereas by American standards the Egyptian had been right in the first place!

In the village, we all rejoiced with those who gained faculty appointments, and suffered with those still waiting. One graduation morning, our song leader arrived for Mass, exclaiming, "He has a job!"—in Kuwait, so (with her parents) we encouraged them to go. The miracle of birth attended us continually; we identified ourselves as "La Leche League" north. Miscarriages would sometimes upset expectations, of course, yet the community rallied. I was particularly impressed with the effect of giving birth on the father, for I had spent my previous sixteen years in men's residence halls, often debating points of faith with bright young men into the wee hours of the morning. But here, when a young man received that emergent child, issues of faith were no longer debating points. Faith became an imperative for young families with so much promise yet so little assurance of the future. Participating in the total shift in orientation that a child brings to new parents could only make me respond with awe and gratitude.

I also learned how ministry is always something shared. The presence of an assistant in ministry helped dramatize that, but in fact any group like ours becomes a community only through the efforts of a half-dozen women who look beyond their own households to help create a nurturing milieu for all. And with sharing comes generosity, so much so that residents would carry a bit of nostalgia for so rich a life amidst such stringent circumstances. We also joked that whoever had lived there for some time would never have to stay in a hotel anywhere in the world. I tested that en route to a medieval Islamic philosophy meeting in Erfurt (in the former East Germany) in 1998. Flying to Budapest, I stayed with a Hungarian couple teaching in Kuwait and home for the summer. We enjoyed together the rich history of that remarkable city. Then on to Krakow to meet a Polish couple who showed me with pride the Jagellonian University, briefing me on the checkered (and often tragic) history of their beautiful country. Krakow's central square is dominated by a striking cathedral, where we were treated to a concert of *Ave Maria*s through the ages on August 15, the feast of the Assumption of Mary. With the soprano voice coming from the choir loft behind, my first-row seat treated me to a sculpted reredos, with Mary expiring in John's arms on the first level, being assumed into heaven in the next, and crowned queen in the top frame. I thought I had died and gone to heaven.

My friends then drove me to Warsaw, by way of Auschwitz and Czestochowa, and then traveling by train to Vienna, where I joined my colleague Gretchen to visit yet another family in lower Austria, before proceeding to Erfurt. That summer I fell in love with Poland, seeing it through the loving eyes of this couple, only to discover how "the wall" had misled us to divide Europe into east and west, while the countries I had visited were more properly "central Europe," with a culture gleaning from both east and west.

If we celebrated countless births in the village, often with baptisms, deaths were always tragic. Here again, it was a privilege to be present to young families in the midst of their trauma. A young couple from Cuttack (Orissa) in India were expecting their second child; he was working seventy miles away in Fort Wayne as an engineer while she was completing her studies in nuclear physics. Returning to work early Monday morning, he swerved to avoid a dog and a car crash suddenly ended his life. Traumatized, we surrounded the pregnant young widow, sitting together with the local Indian community. When her parents arrived to help with the children, her father, Monmohan Chaudury, turned out to be a Gandhi scholar, doggedly continuing the Mahatma's work in India. They stayed through the birth of the baby, and well into toddler stage, while he completed a book on Gandhi and became part of our Kroc Institute seminars. I would later visit them in Cuttack on my next stint in South Asia, finding place on the luggage rack of the Howlah Mail from Calcutta to Bubaniswar, then moving on to participate in a Muslim-Christian study center in Hyderabad, as well as visit our Holy Cross community in Pune. South India offers a far richer panoply of religious diversity than Hindustan.

Another tragedy fully deserves the name: a young Indian couple from the B'nai Israel community in Bombay, a long-standing Jewish presence in South India, arrived in January. They met few people, since the new community center had not yet been built and the playground was filled with snow. The husband failed his doctoral candidacy examination in metallurgical engineering. Though he was told he could retake the exam, he fell into such a depression that he told his only friend in the village to check on the apartment if he did not hear from them in a few days. That friend notified us just after Sunday Eucharist that he had found both husband and wife on the floor of their kitchen, having taken cyanide. Unlike the couple from Orissa, these two were barely known, but the local Reform rabbi (a good friend) responded wholeheartedly, their parents came from Bombay for the burial, and I would later stay with her family on a visit to Pune. Her father was a major in the Indian army while her sister had emigrated to the United States.

One more suicide would traumatize us even more, as we shall see, while other deaths were more poignant than tragic. A woman from the South African Indian community, who had endeared herself to everyone, gave birth as a single parent to a son, whom her mother came to care for. She fast became part of our community as well, yet before long developed pancreatic complications and suddenly died. Advised of the inadequate health care situation in the United States, she had prudently taken out a full policy, which took her body back to South Africa. This story unfolds magically, as a young father in the village found himself suddenly bereft of a wife and mother for their two children, when she suffered a total breakdown. Before long, our single parent had a spouse, and they formed a family with three children. The last trauma on my watch was an infant stillborn to a mother who had had difficulty carrying to term. Active in our small Catholic community, the couple was surrounded by colleagues and friends in the aftermath. Undergoing genetic counseling in the wake of this poignant anticlimax to nine difficult months, they have gone on to a rich family and professional life—indeed rich enough to welcome their latest child with Down's syndrome.

The final two traumas are more personal, the first involving the village intimately, and the second, my Holy Cross confrere John Gerber. The village had a plurality of Chinese families, stemming principally from Father Hesburgh's noticing that key members of the Chinese Academy of Sciences had completed doctoral studies at Notre Dame decades earlier. So when the Cultural Revolution played out, he made contact with them, and we began to receive top science students from China. In fact, we discovered that the number one physics student from China was living with us in the village. From the perspective of ministry, however, the Chinese posed a distinct challenge, starting with manifest cultural differences, including pronouncing their names! (Names provide a fascinating insight into Chinese identity, for they have no difficulty offering us a "Western name," conscious that we find theirs difficult. Fearing this to be ceding to colonialism, I soon realized it was quite the reverse: Chinese have a secure identity, given four thousand years of civilization; they are rather seeking to save us embarrassment!) Moreover, given the Marxist orientation of China, few were Christian, though many seemed interested. We had no proper linguistic access to their community, however, so could at best provide space for a local Chinese evangelical mission. So I was delighted to find that Jean, the spouse of our top physics student, was Catholic, and invited her to assist me in ministry.

Thus began a fruitful relationship from which I learned a great deal as I came to know a marvelous couple. They also helped me gather the Chinese community together one evening, to provide names and addresses of families in Beijing, Shanghai, and Nanjing whom I was able to visit on my return from Bangladesh in 1988. After a few years, however, Jean began showing signs of mental imbalance, which soon escalated into a full-blown emotional breakdown, though not before savagely attacking her husband. We managed to hospitalize her in the local psychiatric ward, just before I was to begin a round of lectures in the east. When I called our solicitous village manager from Washington, she said they felt like "sheep without a shepherd," given Jean's precarious position, which forced me to identify with Jonah! So I canceled everything to return to South Bend, where we were soon to learn that Jean managed to asphyxiate herself with a plastic bag in the psychiatric ward. Once again, I found suicide to be the most taxing of all challenges, humanly and ministerially, for me and for those whom we are called to serve.

Jean's tragedy happened in the fall of 1994. Just one week later my friend John Gerber, not yet sixty-five, told me that a routine biopsy on an unobtrusive swelling in his neck had been positive. He was soon diagnosed with untreatable liver cancer and given six months to live. (I have described the subsequent journey with John in the first chapter of *Friendship and Ways to Truth*, so can be brief here.) A spirituality gleaned from two years with the Navaho, and bolstered by twenty-five years in AA, had taught John how to ask for help, making it possible for us to walk with him. In the last stages of the disease, when he needed assistance to walk, he gave an "open" AA talk in the place he had frequented for twenty-five years, coming up with a line that has directed many of our lives since: "I have come to realize that one lives either by gratitude or resentment; there is no middle ground!"

Having served our community in various roles since our time in Dallas, when he realized that university teaching was not to be his ministry, John always told it like it is. His time with the Navaho people spiced his direction of young men towards priesthood in his role as seminary rector, while the AA tonality to his own life proved especially effective in his various roles as religious superior in our community. He had effectively incorporated women in the staff at our seminary, and on Holy Saturday, the day before he died, five of us were gathered in his room, when he suddenly awoke from a semi-coma to announce, "I am hungry and I need to pee." So another confrere and I spontaneously exited the room to let his women friends take him to the bathroom, utterly chagrined when we realized what we had just done! But our unwitting action also reminded us how women care for us at the beginning and end of life—something John realized full well. In the wake of his death I was able to journey to Europe to renew friendships, in an effort to assimilate our long journey together to the edge, acutely aware that my closest friend had just preceded us on the final journey.

Let me return to the setting of University Village, for I shall always treasure these sixteen years as the richest in my life of ministry. Coming as they did on the cusp of my fiftieth birthday, as my contemporaries were beginning to welcome grandchildren into their lives, I was suddenly granted 150 of them! I had to say goodbye to that ministry, however, when I was invited (in 1997) to spend half of each of the next five years in Jerusalem. Yet handing it on to a confrere, Patrick Gaffney, was a joy. His linguistic and ministerial skills suited him superbly for the task, as he has found similar nourishment in living and serving at University Village.

In the summer of 1998, with the help of a former student and friend, Anne Marie Wolf, I managed to decamp to Moreau Seminary, where I would live with our young Holy Cross members. My presence was appreciated when I could be there, but would not be sorely missed when I had to leave. It has been marvelous coming to know these young men, many of whom I taught in a course in ancient and medieval philosophy, allowing me to introduce them to the Jewish-Christian-Muslim world I was coming to inhabit. I shall describe the last eight years at Notre Dame (1998–2006) in detail in chapter 5, as my center of gravity shifted palpably to Jerusalem. In fact, the years 2004–2006 were entirely spent in the Holy Land. I did manage to return each year the end of Easter week for our Holy Cross ordinations, so in the spring of 2006 we celebrated a blessed transition to emeritus status in both Philosophy and Theology. By then my heart was in Jerusalem, thanks to the university, which had asked me to direct their program at Tantur, and which has also continued to support this daring venture that Father Hesburgh had undertaken at the behest of Paul VI in 1967. So let us move to Jerusalem at this point, fully realizing that it too will be succeeded (though never supplanted) by Uganda.

5

___

Journey to the Holy Land and Early Years There

En route to Jerusalem: Birmingham, Oxford, Cambridge, and Leuven

As NINE YEARS AS chair of theology at Notre Dame came to a close, and I had come to discover how intellectually fruitful exploring Christianity's internal relation to Judaism could be, Father Hesburgh asked me to serve as rector of the Tantur Ecumenical Institute in Jerusalem, rounding out ten years of administration. While the summer spent there in the company of Jewish and Muslim students and scholars in 1975 had endeared me to the place, this year (1980–81) would effectively change my life. What is more, inspired plans for the journey involved flying to the United Kingdom, and proceeding overland to the Holy Land, effecting a liminal transition from administration. A "roots visit" to Edinburgh (whence my father's family had emigrated) allowed me to enjoy the delightful human and intellectual company of Noel Dermot O'Donoghue, an Irish Carmelite theologian whose work I had found invigorating. His area of predilection was Celtic spirituality, yet whatever he touched turned out to illuminate those hearing him or reading his work. Standing high above the Firth of Forth, our conversation somehow turned to the angels. While I should have appreciated that this Celt believed in a lot more than angels, I could not resist a ponderous question (redolent of Karl Rahner): "I cannot help wondering about the soteriological significance of the angels." Noël's retort was immediate: "Hung up on salvation, eh? They're for the glory of God!" (In theological jargon, soteriology is the study of salvation.)

The next stop was Glasgow, to taste the splendid "Burrell collection," where a cousin of my grandfather, who amassed a fortune as a shipbuilder during the Great War, has sought expert help in assembling artifacts from diverse cultures, finally commissioning an Italian architect to display them properly. The polar opposite of most museums, where objects lifted out of context are placed in a large building, this edifice is partitioned into distinct spaces redolent of each culture, giving objects their proper context. One sees many families enjoying this teaching exhibit in the midst of a grand city park.

The Holy Land goal of my pilgrimage then took me to Selly Oak Colleges in Birmingham, where the director of the Christian-Muslim Study Center, David Kerr, helped inaugurate the next and most creative stage of my life of inquiry. A student of world Christianity, David had undertaken the study of Arabic and Islam to that end: how do Christians around the world relate to Islamic societies? Later, David and his wife, Gun, moved to the United States to direct the Duncan Black Macdonald Center for Christian-Muslim Studies at Hartford Seminary. Their hospitality spiced more than one visit to that invaluable resource, named for an enterprising Presbyterian missionary to the Middle East who prepared Christians for a richer understanding of the Islamic culture in which they had chosen to live and work. In the years to come, we would occasionally meet in Jerusalem, on their periodic visits to the Swedish Theological Institute. Some twenty-five years later, David would promote me for an honorary degree at Lund in Sweden, yet only after he had contracted ALS, to which he succumbed just before the ceremony. I was grateful for the opportunity, as it turned out, to spend precious time with his widow, Gun, whose faith and talents, abundantly manifested in creating a home for their family in diverse academic milieus, were pressed to the limit during his last days of relentless physical deterioration.

On a brief stopover in Oxford (in 1980), Fritz Zimmerman welcomed my tentative queries—whether at my age one could begin a study of Islamic thought as it affected Western medieval inquiry—with a hearty: "Come on in! Too many Islamic scholars are philologists who could not recognize a good argument from a bad one; we need philosophers!" Returning to my confrere John Gerber's lair in Cambridge, to visit with

Nicholas and Jan Lash, brought me into initial contact with Rowan Williams, after which we all became dear friends and close collaborators in inquiry. Over the years, Cambridge has never ceased to be a destination for me, as I would return again and again to taste the hospitality of friends with its intellectual vitality. Nicholas Lash arranged a fellowship for me at Clare Hall in the summer of 1989, to complete a translation of al-Ghazali's treatise on the "ninety-nine beautiful names of God." In that connection I met Gray (Aisha) Henry, then directing (with Farid Gouverneur) the Islamic Texts Society. Dedicated to producing well-presented and competent translations of Islamic classics, they had underwritten and agreed to publish this initial attempt at translating from Arabic. We met for tea on the Cam about five, and walked home at ten that evening—friends for life! Gray subsequently returned to her home in Louisville, Kentucky, to care for her aging parents, where before long she began to direct the *Fons Vitae* publishing venture in spirituality, focusing on Sufi Islam and Thomas Merton, later publishing my second translation of al-Ghazali.

At that time (1989), Nicholas Lash's uncle, Sebastian Moore, joined us for a memorable evening at the Lash's, to discuss *Real Presences* with its author, George Steiner. In the course of our subsequent (and wide-ranging) discussion, he queried why Israel had never protested Pol Pot's genocide against his own people. Turning to the State of Israel's continuing occupation and oppression of Palestinians, I asked: "Why should they?" There was an obvious riposte to that, of course, but he caught my point only to acknowledge: "That's why I don't live there." On a later visit to Cambridge (in my role as Director of Studies for our religious community), Charlie Gordon, one of my confreres studying at Cambridge, brought us together with Nicholas and Rosemary Boyle, allowing me to reconnect with Bridget Tighe, an Irish sister who will enter this narrative in the Holy Land.

That was an especially memorable visit, one I had undertaken spontaneously after the untimely death of my closest friend in Holy Cross, John Gerber. Finding a bargain flight to Holland, where I visited friends in Utrecht (whose dissertation I had examined) with their sought-after twins, I went on to celebrate the birthday of my colleague Gretchen Reydams-Schils with their children at Luc's family home in Flanders, then headed to Picardy to spend the 14 July (Bastille Day) weekend with Marie-Louis Siauve, a French translator of al-Ghazali, in their family home—encountering three sets of twin children in the space of one day! "Mimi" had resigned her faculty post in philosophy at Lille in the wake of the Algerian War to serve in a girls' *lycée* in Oran. She came to love Arabic, translating and commenting on the "Book of Love" from al-Ghazali's *magnum opus*, *Ihya' Ulum ad-Din* ("Putting Life Back into Religious Learning"), thereby gaining a second doctorate from the Sorbonne, under the direction of the distinguished Islamicist Roger Arnaldez. Roger had become a good friend through a sister of Holy Cross and student of French literature, Mary Louise Gude, CSC, whose biography of Louis Massignon, the pioneering French Islamicist, is without peer in English (see Epilogue). The daughter of a distinguished physician "who would never have allowed a priest in the house," Mimi confessed that she had begun to pray during the Nazi occupation when her teacher, a priest, had asked her to bring a young woman to refuge in the convent where he was chaplain. When she asked why it had to be during curfew and why she had to do it, he explained, "She's Jewish, of course; and as a woman you can more easily evade curfew." That woman emigrated to the United States after the war, and when Mimi died of cancer a few years after my visit, Irene and I prayed *kaddish* together for her in Skokie, Illinois.

Subsequent visits to Cambridge involved the Margaret Beaufort lecture at the Institute dedicated to teaching of theology for women, at the invitation of Bridget Tighe, who became its director on completing her study of theology, as a "mature student" at Cambridge. Nicholas deLange, an old friend of Nikos Stavroulakis (whom we shall soon meet in more detail) and best known as Amos Oz's translator, invited me to give the Maimonides lecture at the Divinity faculty; and later, Clare College asked me to do the Alma Royalton-Kisch lecture, where Dean Roger Greaves generously provided dinner for all my friends! Catherine Pickstock has become a dear friend as well, and though I regularly prevailed on the hospitality of Jan and Nicholas Lash as well as Rosemary and Nicholas Boyle, Janet Soskice and her artist husband, Oliver, always made room for a stimulating supper with family. Janet and I later collaborated (with Bill Stoeger, SJ, of the Vatican Observatory) to organize a colloquy at Castel Gandolpho on "creation *ex nihilo*" in the Abrahamic faiths. For me, Cambridge means people, and marvelous ones at that, the most recent of whom are Carlo Cogliati, who adroitly shepherded the proceedings of Castel Gandolpho to publication (*Creation and the God of Abraham* [2010]), and Sophia Vasalou, who inspired a colloquy on "wonderment" in the summer of 2008. But let us return to 1980 to resume the journey to Jerusalem, where so much of this took flesh.

Resuming the initial trek to Jerusalem, a brief visit to Leuven, as guest of Frank DeGraeve, SJ, at Heverlée, confirmed my growing project to expand explorations in Jewish-Christian interactions to include Islam. Frank DeGraeve had been a student of Mircea Eliade at the University of Chicago, and later spent a semester each year with us at Notre Dame, to begin to open our theology faculty to "history of religions." As host that evening in Leuven, he had invited two colleagues to supper: his confrere Piet Franssen, SJ, and Jan Walgrave, OP, a distinguished commentator of Aquinas. Having just completed my *Aquinas: God and Action*, I timidly asked Jan Walgrave whether he would consent to review it, and his response—"I just did!"—ushered me into European collegiality. My newfound resolve to study Islam was somehow elicited at Heverlée, revealing a pattern gleaned from Charles Sanders Peirce, who invariably introduces triadic relations to overcome the dualism inherent in bipolar relationships. I had a growing premonition that Jewish-Christian relations, like any bipolar relationship, could easily become stuck, but it would take years in Israel to realize how intractably. So the pilgrimage across Europe to Haifa traversed that continent only to usher me into the multiple worlds of the eastern Mediterranean.

Jerusalem and the Holy Land: Tantur Ecumenical Institute

The last stop on my European overland trek to the Holy Land was a rich encounter with my Notre Dame classmate Nikos Stavroulakis (about whom we shall hear much more) in his Kolonaiki flat in Athens. When the ferry boat for Cyprus and Haifa put in at Piraeus, I was hailed from the upper deck by two of our Holy Cross sisters returning with their van from travel in Italy: Olivette and Carmen, who had inaugurated a study-retreat center in Tiberias on the Sea of Galilee. That encounter proved a salutary omen for subsequent years in the land, as we traversed the Galilee on arrival, to celebrate the feast of the transfiguration of Jesus (August 6) in their house overlooking the Sea of Galilee, marking the close of my first day in the Holy Land only to open unbelievable new vistas. Undertaken initially as a service to our president, Father Hesburgh, that year, together with those that followed upon it organically, if not logically, would be life-transforming for me.

Our experience at Tantur with Jews, Christians, and Muslims in the summer of 1975 had destined me to learn more about Islam, but that needed the time and space of the Mediterranean venue of Tantur to accomplish. Initially, the culturally Jewish milieu of West Jerusalem drew me to the figure of Moses Maimonides, who had been on the periphery of my consciousness since my completion of a study of the philosophical theology of Thomas Aquinas (the aforementioned *Aquinas: God and Action*). On arriving by ferry from Piraeus, I immediately entered an *ulpan*, an Israeli institution for linguistic assimilation, hoping to gain a working knowledge of Hebrew as a stepping-stone to Arabic. I have always been grateful for that strategy for learning Arabic, suggested by some whom I had consulted en route. Mixing with Persian Jews emigrating to Israel in the wake of the Iranian revolution offered me a rich sense of the mosaic of Jewish culture, easily eclipsed in Israel by dominating European (or Ashkenazi) Jews, or in Jerusalem by their black-coated, "ultraorthodox" counterparts. The presence of Sephardic (or "Arab") Jews in an *ulpan* would contrast starkly with their virtual absence among the Israeli intellectuals whom I would later encounter in Hebrew University. The pecking order of this fledgling Israeli society began to emerge, and I became acutely conscious of how it reveals a flaw at the heart of the Zionist dream, intent on making Israel resemble "a bit of Holland" in the Middle East.

Fortunate enough to identify within a few months the person to succeed me as rector at Tantur, a distinguished English Catholic academic and spiritual activist, Donald Nicholl, I was free to relish the inherent advantages of this ecumenical institute, located on a hill between Jerusalem and Bethlehem: a thirty-five acre, walled-in oasis at a checkpoint, poised between the worlds of Israel and Palestine, between Jewish and Muslim majorities. I came to love the place itself, in part because its prescient location meant one dared not overlook either population or cultural group. Moreover, its largely Palestinian staff evidenced a quality of hospitality and dignified long-suffering that would teach me how to jettison my native American optimism for something more theologically tenable: a perduring hope. Over its forty years of existence, countless scholars have discovered what one of its founding lights, Oscar Cullman, found: *Heilsgeographie* ("sacred geography") is as instructive as *Heilsgeschichte* ("salvation history"). My role as rector also introduced me into the "ecumenical" atmosphere of Jerusalem. In the wake of his encounter with the "ecumenical patriarch," Athenagoras, on the Mount of Olives, Paul VI had invited my confrere Theodore Hesburgh to help him respond to the urging of Protestant observers at Vatican II to continue the work of ecumenism by founding an ecumenical institute in Jerusalem, where (in Paul VI's words) "we had all once been one!" Yet as Vatican secretary of state, Montini certainly realized that Christians are nowhere more divided than they are in Jerusalem, so the witness of Tantur would have to be gradual, and for its rector, often exhausting! For me, the posturing of ecclesiastics in Jerusalem, often without substantive communities to serve, offered a glimpse of the major pitfall of progress in ecumenism: property. (Karl Marx would have predicted that as well, of course.)

So I would find the immensely rich panoply of interfaith exchange, already tasted between generations at our Tantur gathering in 1975, to be far more promising than ecclesiastical jealousies. And as the following year of study was to reveal, the subject of my recent study, Thomas Aquinas, had found critical inspiration from Jewish as well as Islamic thinkers for his sustained project of showing how "sacred doctrine" could be a proper "mode of knowing." Yet generations of Western students of his thought had neglected to follow his citation trail and to notice the role these Jewish and Muslim thinkers played in his work. It would take the Mediterranean perspective of Jerusalem, and then of Cairo, to show how that acknowledged synthesis of Christian theology, Aquinas' *Summa Theologiae*, already represented an intercultural, interfaith achievement. I would need a few more years to show that, beginning the following year (1981–82), in the supportive Dominican milieu of Isaiah House in Jerusalem, with the inspiring presence of Marcel Dubois, OP (d. 2007), soon to be followed by the Institut Dominicain d'Etudes Orientales in Cairo, with its commanding presence, Georges Anawati, OP (d. 1994).

But the Holy Land, which captivated my psyche after my initial years there, had much more to offer than an intellectual agenda. Two years opened a geographical and interpersonal space that would prove enlarging and life-sustaining. Taken together, they offered a stereoscopic view of the land as home to two peoples, with Tantur facing Bethlehem and the West Bank, and Isaiah House, on the edge of West Jerusalem, explicitly focused on the Jewish people. The first year at Tantur brought me into official contact with Christian ecclesial presence, and more interestingly with scholars tracing the meaning of the land, notably for Christians.

Simon Schoon, with his wife, Riet, brought their family to Tantur from Holland, and later in the year adopted an Ethiopian toddler—starkly contrasting with his utterly blonde Dutch sisters! In my estimation, families gained most from Tantur, as the children attended the Anglican school (a mini-United Nations) and spouses found volunteer work in Bethlehem—renewal for the whole family! In fact, spouses gained Arabic faster in the market than scholars in their study. Connection with the Jewish world that year came largely through conferences and the "Rainbow," a venerable interfaith group, whereas the following year would see me teaching at Hebrew University, while Simon returned to Holland to direct Jewish-Christian relations as well as pastor for the Reformed church. Tantur scholars (with families) profited from excursions directed by knowledgable historians and archaeologists, so the year confirmed Cullman's sense that Tantur's very location would contribute to developing a sense for "sacred geography." In fact, Christian theologians who have studied at Tantur gained something that a superb European library is unable to supply. Yet the Tantur library itself has been assiduously developed over the years, initially by the resident community of monks from Montserrat, who assured that it contained a core of classical texts and prominent reference works. Subsequent expansion, notably in English monographs, has brought it to the point of being the best theological library in the Middle East. And while it cannot claim to be a university research facility, rich holdings in patristics and primary theological sources from Protestant and Catholic traditions offer a splendid resource, notably in conjunction with the serene setting.

The Galilee became a mecca for me, in stark contrast to the "holy sites" in Jerusalem, which often demanded the expertise of an archaeologist to decipher thanks to centuries of accumulated debris. In the Galilee, however, Jesus' presence seems to suffuse everything. Mater Ecclesia Center, established by our Holy Cross sisters some years before on the shore of the lake to offer biblical and spiritual formation to sisters from the developing world, became a special attraction to me. Their nine-month program ended with Holy Week in Jerusalem, when a two-month program for expatriate sisters serving in the Middle East took up. It became a monthly pilgrimage to connect with our community, and to bask in an unobstructed view of the Golan Heights. Sister Olivette directed my retreat each year in the fall, during Jewish holy days, and I would lead the expatriate sisters in the Gospel of John for a week after Easter. That is where I met Bridget Tighe, a missionary Franciscan from Ireland, in the throes of founding a clinic for Palestinian women in Zarka, north of Amman in Jordan. Nurse and midwife, Bridget exuded a spontaneous receptivity that was infectious. Through her I came to know their remarkable community in Amman, visiting whenever I needed to breathe more freely. While the Israel of the early eighties seemed fairly calm, with the "occupation" reputedly benign, rumblings were evident to anyone with local friends, so an interlude in Amman could prove liberating. I distinctly remember having been unable to compose an article on "the situation" requested by *Commonweal*, yet completing it in a morning at the sisters' house in Amman, while they were out serving Palestinian families.

Isaiah House

As the rectorship in Tantur came to an end, I received the promised sabbatical, so contracted with Marcel Dubois to reside at Isaiah House the following year. A quick trip to Cairo to meet Father Anawati and the French Dominicans confirmed that it could have been more advantageous to spend the next year with them, but having fallen in love with Jerusalem, I cast my lot in that place guaranteed to break one's heart. Yet it proved serendipitous, as we shall see, to follow my heart, while Cairo would later occupy a number of summers. My initial encounter with Anawati was immensely encouraging. Approaching the venerable scholar hat in hand, I asked him if he thought I could do what I intended: enter sufficiently into Arabic to retool into Islamic philosophy. How was he, or anyone, to answer a question like that; but his pastoral side prevailed, and his encouraging response was all I needed: "It will be difficult, but I believe you can do it." That his words proved true testifies to his mentorship in the upcoming years. Abouna Anawati would preside at table with the community and welcome residents into his study to ponder texts during the day. His presence was always refreshing, and his guidance gently demanding. One always felt he knew much more than he let on, but that bespeaks a good teacher: leading students by the hand to help them go on. A deeply spiritual person, his life was for people, his work neat with no nonsense. He made the richness of his person available to all, while maintaining a resolute fidelity to community prayer and camaraderie. Jean-Jacques Perrenès, OP, the prior who moved the house and the institute forward after the loss of Anawati, has done him justice in a recent monograph: *Georges Anawati: Un chrétien égyptien devant le mystère de l'Islam* (2008).

In the meantime, I had moved into Isaiah House, in West Jerusalem, with Marcel Dubois and a small Dominican community, including Frère Jacques Fontaine, who had guided our pilgrimage to the land in 1975. A master of Hebrew and of the Bible, he had made the land come alive for us and for many others, while now his dry humor made him a joy to live with. Traveling in open jeeps—men and women, Jews, Christians, and Muslims—each of us had at least two languages, so could facilitate communication with more than one partner. When we came to a biblical site, Frère Jacques would open his pocket-size *Bible de Jerusalem* to recite the text. For temporary relief en route, men went to one side of the large jeep and women to the other; nights were on the ground: hence "Bible sur terrain."

When I arrived to stay in 1981, however, it was Marcel who became friend and mentor, with exemplary fidelity to our daily prayer (in Hebrew), especially as he treasured night hours for work or to celebrate friendships with an extensive Jerusalem community. A philosopher with a mystical bent, he was ever exploring the theological rift that history had opened between the two covenants—indeed, living therein and tasting both affinities and differences. My budding desire to complement Jewish-Christian understanding with that of Islam began with a sabbatical year devoted to Moses Maimonides, as well as undertaking Arabic with Ibrahim Yannon, a stimulating mentor at Hebrew University, where Marcel Dubois was serving as chair of philosophy. He arranged for me to offer a seminar in Maimonides and Aquinas in the spring term, which helped defray my Arabic instruction, as well as launch a systematic exploration of Thomas Aquinas' reliance on Jewish and Islamic philosophers, as they all searched for ways to articulate creation *ex nihilo*. Immersed as he had been in the "Islamicate," Maimonides proved to be the perfect bridge-figure to initiate an intellectual journey to be continued with George Anawati and the Dominican community in Cairo, directing what would become a quarter-century immersion in Jewish-Christian-Muslim interaction in the medieval period—with inevitable contemporary resonances. In this way, the sabbatical year at Isaiah House would bear fruit exceeding any expectations. But that is what liminal space portends, and what the growing friendship with Marcel augured.

Indeed, I suspect that our mutual resonance—philosophical and religious—germinated a theme that would later serve to unite a series of essays published under the title *Friendship and Ways to Truth* (2000). Yet philosophers normally show respect for one another in contentious ways, so we would regularly clash over Marcel's quite abstract way of referring to "Arabs," as well as what I took to be his excessively poetic optic on "Israel." My year at Tantur had introduced me to countless Palestinian friends, alerting me to the hazards inherent in Israeli occupation, unfailingly displayed at checkpoints. And while Tantur's location "between the worlds" had proved to be its prime asset, the Old City's Jaffa Gate was a mere five minutes up Agron Street from Isaiah House, a walk easy to negotiate but one that Marcel seldom took. His sights were set on Mount Scopus and Hebrew University. Similarly, his French Dominican confreres at Ecole Biblique on Nablus Road were but fifteen minutes away, yet the two houses proved to be worlds apart.

The story of Marcel's own "conversion from his naive Zionism," as he came to put it, would be played out after Isaiah House no longer formally existed. Michel Sabbagh, the first Arab Latin patriarch, invited him to participate (as a Catholic priest with Israeli citizenship) in a theological commission to explore interfaith relations in the politically conflicted space of the Holy Land and especially Jerusalem, so Marcel came to enter Jaffa Gate frequently, and before long was fraternally welcomed to Ecole Biblique as well. That takes us ahead of the story of Isaiah House as liminal space, yet while his own journey could hardly have been predicted in 1982, it may have begun to germinate in our contentious debates regarding Palestine and Israel during that intense year. For besides coming to a potent appreciation of the philosophical and pedagogical skills of the Rambam (the Hebrew acronym for *R*abbi *M*oses *b*en *M*aimon), the seminar instigated by Marcel was to uncover the role "Rabbi Moses" played in helping forge Aquinas' *Summa Theologiae*, opening the way for me to show how that acknowledged classical synthesis of Christian theology already represented an intercultural, interfaith achievement. So while Marcel himself remained relatively untutored in Islamic philosophy, his suggesting that I focus on Moses Maimonides as a complementary figure to Aquinas in fact directed the rest of my life of scholarship. He would prove to have a similar effect on the intellectual life of many.

And that effect also had a way of transcending the limitations of the specifically Ashkenazi culture that Marcel had in fact adopted, quite oblivious to its intellectual limitations. For moving in the Israeli academic circles that he so thoroughly enjoyed, and that reciprocated in kind, "Jewish" simply meant "Ashkenazi," by an implicit identification of which Marcel would be oblivious. If he had been encouraged to follow up the implications of Moses Maimonides' immersion in what Marshall Hodgson has called "the Islamicate," he would have discovered a Judaism imbued with a philosophical sophistication imbibed from Islamic culture, and so be led to discover Aquinas afresh as well. In this respect, he was doubly betrayed—by his well-meaning Dominican mentors in France, who had barely mentioned Aquinas' Islamic interlocutors, and by his Israeli academic hosts, whose European culture effectively suppressed the intellectual perspectives of Jewish compatriots enriched by Islamic culture. In fact, calling attention to this fault line in Israeli academic culture has effects even more neuralgic than uncovering their endemic denial of Palestinian occupation, for the latter can be exposed by standard "human rights" language, while recalling the Ashkenazi-Sephardic divide can open seething cultural antagonisms. Marcel would be brought to realize how sequestered his life had been, yet through human contact with devout Muslims, acute testimony to his profound human receptivity, a trait that found expression in his abiding capacity for friendship. So together with his student and, later, colleague and companion, Avital Wohlman, Marcel became another significant mentor to me on the journey to becoming a lover.

Through it all, the liminal space of Isaiah House uncannily prepared me to appreciate the ways in which Jewish-Christian understanding would require opening to Muslim interlocutors to realize its potential. The proximity of Isaiah House to the Ratisbonne Institute for Jewish-Christian Studies helped make this point, albeit in a reactive way. As I participated in programs there, with the intent of understanding better the practicalities of Jewish-Muslim relations, I was appalled at the ways in which Christian participants could be preoccupied with the niceties of Ashkenazi Judaism. One can respect such hair-splitting within traditions, yet also celebrate the fact that belonging to another tradition frees one from them. Yet among many Christians at Ratisbonne, the opposite proved to be the case. Moreover, in an institute dedicated to respect for Jewish tradition, I found a correlative tendency to emphasize one's respect for Judaism by one's endorsement of Zionism, as though the two were synonymous. Fortunately, my Israeli friends who thought otherwise kept me from being distracted by these internecine debates. Yet all this conspired to reinforce the convictions of the American philosopher C. S. Peirce that a propensity to think in triads helps neutralize bipolar thinking, alerting me to realize how easily bipolar relationships can become stuck (as the demand for marriage counselors strongly suggests)! So experience of its conspicuous absence in Israeli life brought me to see how sensible and necessary Muslim presence can be to interfaith dialogue.

Again, little of this stemmed from Marcel Dubois himself, yet most of it can readily be attributed to the milieu he helped create at Isaiah House, and notably to a faith in the presence of God that his witness exuded. Though Catholic to the core, so natively inclined to interpret any world—Jewish as well as Christian—through a sacramental vision, Marcel never imposed that perspective on others in a hegemonic way. His intellectual breadth combined with a Catholic aversion to proselytizing to exude tolerance: "We learn how to agree to disagree in our approaches to God." Monthly seminars with Yesheyahu Leibovitz at Isaiah House witnessed to the breadth of his intellectual receptivity, and proved to be a veritable seedbed for intellectual exchange across traditions. A physical chemist and a philosopher, Professor Leibowitz had served as editor-in-chief of the Israeli Encyclopedia, and in the wake of the Six-Day War in 1967 had morphed from professor to prophet, shouting, "Give it back!" His argument was thoroughly Zionist, in clear contrast to Martin Buber and Judah Magnes, inspiring leader of Hebrew University. While they had argued for a "binational" state, he insisted that the state be Jewish, since (in a proper nineteenth-century optic) a state is the vehicle needed to promote culture, and he was intent on promoting Jewish culture. Yet while everyone realized that incorporating the people in the land occupied in 1967 would spell the demographic demise of a Jewish state, he took the discussion a step further, noting that ruling over people whom Israel refused to incorporate into their body politic assured it could not ethically be a Jewish state. Israel has been living with that contradiction ever since, doing what we all do with contradictions of this potency—namely, deny it, much as America did with slavery, where our Declaration was contradicted by the constitutional compromise that slaves shall count as three-fifths of a person.

What brought this unlikely pair of mentors together was respect for their own traditions, and pain at their inevitable distortions. A key participant in Isaiah House and the dialogue with Leibovitz, in particular, was Avital Wohlman (whom we shall encounter later as Tali), whose acute philosophical wit and utterly refined sensibility would continue to attract and haunt me. Marcel never ceased to give witness to a sacramental vision of Judaism as well as Christianity, in his relations with others and especially through unstinting friendships. Some years later, during a short visit to Jerusalem from Cairo, I enjoyed supper with Marcel and Tali at Mishkenot sh'Anim, a restaurant frequented by Jerusalem elite. Still struggling with the relation between the two covenants, I thanked Marcel for having inducted me into the Jewish sensibility needed to follow Jesus, yet I had also come to realize that without Jesus, the Hebrew Scriptures seemed to lack focus, as they could be twisted like a wax nose by any group. His response: "Of course!" So simple!

In the meantime, the vision of the "mystery of Israel" elicited by his poetic and theological sensibilities would be continually belied by the actions of the Jewish state. And when we recall that he had become an intentional citizen of Israel, who was later to receive the coveted Israel Prize, the dissonance between his theological vision of the return of the Jewish people to *eretz Israel*, and the actions of a state intent on occupying another people to keep hold of that land, was bound to escalate in ways that would prove to be unsupportable. As an American I had to learn from the conflict in the Holy Land how to distill the theological virtue of hope from a native optimism; while Marcel, as a French Catholic, would be brought to sunder the attachment evidenced by his Catholic compatriots, Charles Peguy and Jacques Maritain, to the venture of Israel, by employing a theology of history astute enough to assess sociopolitical realties for what they are. Given his love for the Jewish people with whom he lived and worked, as well as his profound theological vision of the "mystery of Israel," so painful a detachment would take time, but in a mind and soul as single-minded towards truth as Marcel's, it was bound to come. This interior journey of conversion has been delineated by his younger confrere Olivier-Thomas Venard, from a prolonged set of interviews with Marcel: *La nostalgie d'Israel* (2004), translated by Mary Louise Gude, CSC, as *The Israel We Longed For: Reflections of Marcel Dubois O.P.* (in search of a publisher).

A Key Transition: Donald Nicholl—Beyond Administration at Notre Dame, with Life in Tantur

I was to trek from Isaiah House to Tantur each *shabbat* to lunch with Donald Nicholl and Dorothy, for the ten-year advance he had on me, together with his depth of experience and analytic acumen, indicated that he could be the spiritual mentor and guide I needed for the transition overtaking me, which was intimately related to Notre Dame. Father Hesburgh had come to visit early in my initial year at Tantur, and when he wanted to see Ben-Gurion's tomb in the Negev, we set off in a Volkswagen, enjoying the bracing landscape of the desert. En route, we stopped for lunch in a "settlement town"—a bleak locale to which immigrants from places other than Europe were sent. We noticed a group of blacks hanging around the simple restaurant, so I quickly gave Ted a breakdown of the Israeli pecking order: First, Ashkenazi Jews from Europe, then Sephardic Jews from Arab lands, and lastly, Falasha Jews from Ethiopia. Greeting them as we entered, Ted said: "Hi, guys! Where are you from?" "Gary" was the answer! We had stumbled on members of a sect from America, the "Black Hebrews," soon to be ejected from Israel for human rights violations toward their own.

Journeys together can help break through fixed relationships—in this case, faculty member and university president—and cement friendship between confreres, albeit sixteen years apart. And I have no doubt that this visit did, as did a journey we had taken together to Salamanca for an International Federation of Catholic Universities meeting in 1972, and yet another to Puerto Alegre, Brazil, just three years before (1978). Yet this visit also made me realize that I need not be preoccupied with succeeding him as president of Notre Dame—which can easily become an indoor sport at a place as insular as Notre Dame, and was particularly seductive to younger, brighter members of the Holy Cross community. Three *B*s had been touted for the job: Ernie Bartell, Jim Burtchaell, and myself. How did I come to know this aspiration was "null and void"? I cannot say, but somehow the message was conveyed to me, so I had to process it.

Letting it drop proved to release me from an albatross, but it would take Donald Nicholl's presence and frequent conversations together to allow that to happen. I knew I had always been oriented to older brothers, given the configuration of our family, and Ted had easily filled that psychic space. So coming to the realization that I was not the "heir apparent" left space for another "older brother," into which Donald fit handily. And I should really say "Donald and Dorothy," for she clearly kept Donald rooted, and her presence at Tantur offered that feminine sensibility (with good sense!) that Vivi Siniora would later bring. In fact, having raised a family to the point where they were on their own, Dorothy just continued caring as she always had! Donald brought the critical edge of an Oxford historian to everything, along with the irrepressible appetite of a generalist, who had taken a summer to learn Russian so as to apprentice himself to Hesychast spiritual masters. Yet beneath it all was the no-nonsense grounding of a "Yorkshire man," ever alert to the plight of miners and the travails of ordinary folk who must grub for a living. His military service in South Asia during the Second World War gave him a resonance with interior disciplines, which he translated to everyday actions like eating and breathing—a natively Zen sensibility.

Donald became my spiritual mentor that year, though when he contracted cancer years later (in the wake of my close friend John Gerber), he would not let me visit him—"David, what if I am really down when you spend all that money to come? Besides, we both know we shall meet in a much better place. In the meantime I am resting here, gazing at icons and pictures of friends—the same thing, really—with Dorothy to care for me." So I called monthly to speak with them, yet when Donald finally succumbed, Dorothy and the family organized a public memorial in Farm Street Church in London. So when she asked me to come, for she had orchestrated a group representative of diverse eras of Donald's life, apologizing that it was to speak for ten minutes on his life at Tantur, I responded with alacrity. When the editor of the *Tablet* reminded us that Donald had just completed ninety-nine articles for that Catholic journal, all present allowed that anything he wrote proved insightful. But the best recommendation for Donald came from Henry Chadwick, when I had put forth Donald for rector in a Tantur Advisory Council meeting in 1980. As we scrutinized Donald's *curriculum vitae*, a German scholar wondered whether he was "scholarly enough" for the role, so I nudged Henry, only to hear him respond: "Nicholl! Nicholl's no fool!" I had to explain to the Bavarian that this was Oxbridge's highest encomium! While my next steps would lead to Cairo before long, let me pause here to try to capture what Tantur has come to mean to so many.

6

Focus on Tantur, Cairo, and Hania

Twenty-five Years of Tantur

THE INITIAL YEAR IN Jerusalem (1980–81) suggests how the intellectual and emotional domain that opened to me in the last quarter-century began to take shape: "Jewish-Christian-Muslim interaction in the medieval period," usually adding that Jerusalem immediately catapults one into the world in which we live. The Jewish sector of that world has been Israel, from the vantage point of a thirty-five acre, walled-in oasis just inside Jerusalem at the Bethlehem checkpoint. A magnificent location for interfaith study, this Christian residential facility with a superb theological library could serve as an icon of the community of Christians in the Holy Land, squeezed, as it were, between two majorities, with one of these still thinking of itself as a minority, which complicates the issue. Yet the effects of that pressure have become painfully evident in the twenty-five years since my intermittent sojourn at Tantur began in 1980. Two *intifadas* (Palestinian uprisings) have intervened since then, with considerable hardening on the Israeli side, notably of a virulent "religious" sort. Settlers, once "secular," have become fanatically "religious," insisting that God gave *us* this land, with the mandate to fight anyone else's encroachment on what is by right *ours*. (Their favorite biblical book is Joshua!) Ordinary land tenure issues are summarily trumped, and residents "from time immemorial" brutally ejected from their land by settler militias, while regular Israeli army or police conveniently step aside ("They are Jews; how can we oppose them?").

Thanks to a vigorous local press, notably the English edition of the daily *Ha-aretz* (Israel's *Manchester Guardian*), one is treated to sustained discussion of the issues besetting the State of Israel, including and especially the collective denial of the ongoing illegal and repressive occupation. But conversations with Israelis—even devotees of *Ha-aretz*—regularly trade in euphemisms like "the situation," as a sign of ongoing denial as well as a kind of moral fatigue at their nation's inability to carry out what has to be the prime strategic interest of Israel: ending the occupation to give space to a viable Palestinian state next door. Ever since the celebrated "handshake on the White House lawn" in 1993, which opened a window of hope, Israel has been endemically unwilling to treat Palestinians like fellow human beings, keeping security and economic reins tightly in their hands. When the frustration erupted in a desperation tactic of suicide bombings of public transport, the apoplectic fear that seized Israeli society moved the political powers to a policy of separation, now set in concrete barriers eight meters high.

Christian communities both in Palestine and in Israel, though politically powerless, nonetheless offer a witness—through their presence in education, health care, and numerous social services—which far outstrips their diminutive minority status. A sizable number continue to be expatriates, evoking a presence established in the last quarter of the nineteenth century, when a weak Ottoman regime allowed Western powers to establish a presence in Palestine, with the result that Christian children came to enjoy a superior education, later extended to Muslim children as well. Hence the temptation peculiar to Christians to emigrate in the face of deplorable prospects for employment in a Palestinian economy, or palpable discrimination at Israeli checkpoints, especially when countless members of the extended family have already emigrated to other countries, beginning in 1948. Statistically, the prospect looks bleak for Christians, fractured for Muslims in the face of various Islamist initiatives, and disillusioning for Jews, as the Zionist dream has devolved into a nightmare. Yet in the face of all of that, valiant voices and creative initiatives on all sides stir a deeply rooted hope for some kind of *modus vivendi*. It is as though the worse things get, the more one seeks for ways through the apparent impasse. As with most polities in our world today, political figures seem to conspire to betray the hopes of their people, whose aspirations are the same the world over: to feed, raise, and educate their families.

Yet in the midst of all this, and perhaps inspired by it, friendships flourish. Beyond the sustaining cohort at Tantur, Jerusalem yields a sturdy group of people with whom one could walk the walk in the midst of injustice and unrest. We have already met one to whom I was closest, Marcel Dubois, OP. I then began to team teach philosophy at Hebrew University with his former student and subsequent colleague, Avital Wohlman, with whom he came to share so much of his life. Tali and I began working together on many things Islamic as I would later translate (from French to English) her rendition of the celebrated standoff between al-Ghazali and Averroës (*Al-Ghazali, Averroes and the Interpretation of the Qur'an: Common Sense and Philosophy in Islam* [2009]). We may continue to disagree as to which of them related faith with reason in a more nuanced way, yet her limpid philosophical prose challenged me to produce an adequate English rendering. We became especially close as Marcel was steadily failing, to the point of Tali's taking him to Hadassah Hospital on Mount Scopus for multiple tests and observation, only to have him soon slip away in his sleep (in June 2007). Tali, collaborating with a colleague and friend, Yossi Schwartz, published a collection of essays limning Marcel Dubois' polyvalent contributions to intellectual life in Jerusalem. Yossi had introduced himself to me in the medieval philosophy meeting in Erfurt in 1998 as "Tali's student," which immediately opened a friendship. That encounter was sealed in the midst of a celebratory roast in the castle overlooking Erfurt, when Yossi learned of the death of his uncle in New York. He needed a Hebrew bible to send condolences to the family, and I was able to produce one from the library in the seminary where I was staying. Interfaith relations proceed "one friendship at a time," as my late colleague Michael Signer avowed and our colleagueship exemplified.

Mustafa Abu-Sway (whose family lives in East Jerusalem on Ras al-Amud) has been a friend and dialogue partner for decades, along with Yeheskel Landau, whom I first met in the Hope Seminar in 1975, and with whom I edited *Voices from Jerusalem* (1991), a collection of interfaith testimonies manifesting how and why Jerusalem could have sufficient consistency to be the capital of two states. A "religious educator," Yeheskel had to leave Israel during the second intifada (2000) and currently teaches in Hartford Seminary in Connecticut, focusing on Jewish-Muslim dialogue, where the one-hundredth anniversary celebration of the periodical *Muslim World* brought us together again in 2010. We shall hear more of Mustafa in the Epilogue.

Christian institutions in Bethlehem and Jerusalem are populated by religious communities of men and of women with incredible staying power, serving Jewish and Muslim worlds with that special institutional witness that Catholics do so well. To walk onto the campus of Bethlehem University is to encounter vibrant young people (70 percent Muslim, 62 percent women); a stark contrast to the manifest reduction of Bethlehem itself in the face of the eight-meter wall prohibiting passage to Jerusalem, with access to its educational and health care institutions. The community of De La Salle Christian Brothers, with a sterling lay staff—many, their own graduates with advanced degrees from abroad— have managed to keep doors open during recurrent sieges, and spirits hopeful in the face of countless Israeli incursions. Their spirit has created a milieu in which young people—Muslim and Christian, men and women—can envisage a future in otherwise quite hopeless surroundings. An unparalleled witness to the gospel with steady resistance to occupation, this university is in many ways the heart of present-day Bethlehem. Peter deBrul, SJ, has graced the university with his formidable intellectual and spiritual presence for years, currently continued by that of Jamal Khader, a priest of the Jerusalem patriarchate, whose presence regularly spans the worlds to include Hebrew University. Whenever I come to the Holy Land, I make a point of communing with Peter on recent French philosophical works and other precious things, and shall never forget his introducing me to René Girard's *Des choses caches depuis la fondation du monde* in 1981 in Jerusalem.

Another such witness can be found on the other side of Jerusalem, in Ein Karem, the traditional village of Elizabeth and Zachary, where a core group of Daughters of Charity, assisted by medical personnel and European volunteers, cares for profoundly handicapped Israeli and Palestinian children. This international community prays in French, as do many Holy Land communities, and consists of sisters from Lebanon, Austria, Philippines, Italy, and the United States. Again, these unique modes of institutional presence exemplify the witness that Christians can and do give. A final example, the Christian Peacemaker Team (CPT) in Hebron, is utterly dedicated to nonviolence in a city whose modern history bespeaks violence fueled by virulent religious hatred, largely located in small but truculent Jewish enclaves bisecting the old city of Hebron, itself an architectural gem. CPT volunteers accompany Palestinian children who must pass by these aggressive enclaves walking to and from class. Christian groups like these become a destination for visitors to Jerusalem, to lead them "beyond the sound bites" to meet courageous persons of faith.

Remarkable people from many countries live and work in an institute surrounded by a garden in the midst of East Jerusalem: Ecole Biblique et Archaeologique Française. A Dominican foundation, scholars from "the Ecole" produced *The Jerusalem Bible* in the sixties, originated the scholarship on the Dead Sea Scrolls, and have created a challenging and supportive community for students from various lands. Many friends here over the years have sustained my intellectual and spiritual life in Jerusalem, but none so tellingly as Olivier-Thomas Venard, OP. His creative work in Thomas Aquinas has opened up new vistas in his philosophical theology, precisely by focusing on the poetic structure of his language. Startling as it is to be comparing Aquinas' prose with Rimbaud's poetry, Olivier-Thomas makes a powerful case by illuminating the potential of linguistic strategies for philosophical theology. This intellectual energy has recently been channeled into a fresh presentation of *The Jerusalem Bible*, if you will, which seeks to reincorporate patristic and other commentaries into an edition of the bible with text surrounded by classical commentary, in a fashion not unlike the classical Jewish commentary by Rashi. Our friendship has blossomed into fascinating colloquies—one in Oxford in 2006 (on "light" with John Milbank and Catherine Pickstock); another in Tantur in 2007, organized by Jim Heft, with an astute group of younger Jews, Christians, and Muslims seeking new pathways in interfaith dialogue; and again in Nottingham (in 2010) to celebrate the life and work of Fergus Kerr, OP. The quality of encounter possible in the context of religious communities like those in Jerusalem or Cairo gives testimony to something outside the ordinary ambit of friendship, adding a new dimension of exchange.

Of many other Jerusalem luminaries and friends, some work for NGOs, like Hanna Siniora and Gershon Baskin with the Israel-Palestine Committee for Research and Information, located at Tantur where Israeli and Palestinian staff work tirelessly for peace in the face of unimaginable obstacles. Still others served the Lutheran World Federation, Worldvision, or Catholic Relief Services, spending discrete periods of service and enriching our lives in succession. Tom and Karen Getman (of Worldvision) taught me the potency of evangelical prayer to spice trenchant analyses of "the situation," while Craig and Lois Kippels (of LWF) punctuated our week during the Gulf War crisis by sponsoring (with Guido Gockel, MHM, of Catholic Near East Welfare Association [NY]) a "thank God it's Friday" gathering at an East Jerusalem trattoria. We all needed one another's support, once we realized how we Americans were at the heart of the problem! (Just to show how ubiquitous NGO executives can be, Craig and Lois subsequently showed up in Uganda, where we spent three years together.) An Israeli from the South African Jewish community, Lynda Brayer, who found her way to the Catholic Church, partly in protest to the unremitting legal positivism at Hebrew University Law School, went on to found the Society of St. Yves to carry the battle against occupation to the courts, notably fighting house demolition in the Israeli High Court. We became dear friends for nearly a decade, before her own journey took her out of the fray, into a Buddhist retreat in Florida and back to Haifa. I learned from Lynda that anger cannot be the last word, even when anger is the only rational response to injustice—something she became used to encountering daily.

One family deserves special mention, however, whom I first met through Lynda: Jihad Hamad, who would marry Manar (also from Beit Hanoun in Gaza), returned from Notre Dame to live with their five children in Gaza, though were more recently liberated to Canada. Jihad had followed the route of many Palestinians to undertake Peace Studies at Notre Dame: Bethlehem University, with an interlude in an Israeli prison, followed by serving in the kitchen at Tantur. He showed acute organizational ability in the deliberate mix of international students brought to Notre Dame for Peace Studies, including a Palestinian and an Israeli, a Turk and a Kurd. Living together, they learned about reconciliation at many levels of interaction. Jihad went on to pursue a doctorate in sociology after returning to Beit Hanoun (in Gaza) upon obtaining his MA, in the company of a young wife, Manar. She immediately obtained her GED, enrolled in Indiana University (South Bend) for a BA, endearing herself to everyone living in University Village as they named their first child Salaam (Peace). On the death of Israeli Prime Minister Yitzhak Rabin, assassinated by a radical religious settler, Jihad came with me to the local synagogue memorial service. The rabbi, a good friend, introduced him to the congregation, and when he informed them that they had named their firstborn son Salaam (making

Jihad and Manar Abu-Salaam and Umm-Salaam, respectively), he was embraced by the entire Beth Israel congregation.

Upon completion of his PhD, Jihad gained a faculty post at a new Palestinian university near Jenin, in the West Bank. Visiting them there, during a conversation with students in the cafeteria, Jihad and I spoke so easily about matters Catholic or Muslim that this predominantly Muslim student group wondered how he knew so much about Christianity. He remarked that he was "sort of a Catholic Muslim," to which I retorted, "I guess I am a sort of Muslim Catholic." I was convinced that before long he would become dean at the fledgling Arab-American University, which employed English instruction on the model of American University in Beirut. But family responsibilities demanded he visit Beit Hanoun to attend his father for a surgical operation, and Israeli authorities would not permit him to return to Jenin. In the event, Manar had sorely missed her family, so returned with the children to Gaza, where they continued to reside, with two more children and with Jihad teaching at al-Azhar University, and regularly interviewed by al-Jazeera. I visited them whenever I could make arrangements to do so, usually through Catholic Relief Services. When I spoke with them by telephone, after one more disastrous occurrence in Gaza, Jihad would respond with the vibrant faith in God that keeps them all alive. Before long, however, nightly shocks from Israeli jets gratuitously breaking the sound barrier drove the family to desperation, and a fortunate collusion of circumstances (plus immense pluck) allowed them to leave though Rafah for Cairo (where his brother lives as a physician) and thence to London, Ontario, where he is teaching sociology at a Canadian university as they raise a family in multicultural exile.

Notre Dame Student Program at Tantur

Donald Nicholl made extensive contacts with Israeli and Palestinian intellectuals, helping Tantur fulfill the "bridging" location its mission calls for, yet also faced the fact that the facility had been constructed on a scale too large for the number of scholars one might reasonably expect to come. On the one hand, despite their rhetoric, academics are normally not that adventuresome; and on the other, Tantur had no fellowships to offer to facilitate individuals or families coming. We had counted on sabbatical leaves, and were soon told that that expectation was entirely too American. So Donald concocted programs of continuing education, beginning with the Maryknoll Mission Society of America, and gradually extending to all comers, men and women, Protestant, Orthodox, and Catholic. There was predictable resistance on the part of those dedicated to a facility for scholars, including the sterling small community of monks from Montserrat, who had been an integral part of Father Hesburgh's original vision: scholars study while monks pray. Yet sad as it was to see them go (with many factors affecting their decision), one fringe benefit of their departure was that scholars and other participants had to do both! Landrum Boling, who succeeded Donald Nicholl, had served as president of Earlham College in Indiana, so immediately saw the potential for an undergraduate program of study at Tantur.

On his advice, Notre Dame launched such a program in 1986. A priest from Baltimore with a doctorate in counseling from Notre Dame, Dennis Madden, served as the initial director of the student program. He later moved into Jerusalem to direct the Palestine Mission of the Catholic Near East Society (for the archdiocese of New York), and still later was appointed auxiliary bishop in Baltimore. Dennis arranged a program engaging students with the sociopolitical situation through meeting ordinary Palestinians, including those displaced in refugee camps in or near Bethlehem, leading them in substantive reflection on what they experienced. When Dennis moved on, Mary Aquin O'Neill, RSM, welcomed students into a stimulating experience, yet before long the university felt the need to engage regular faculty in the program, asking Patrick Gaffney, CSC, a professor in anthropology fluent in Arabic, to direct it for a year. He utilized his extensive contacts in the Jerusalem area to exploit Israeli and Palestinian resources from the area, to offer students the analytic tools needed to assess what they encountered daily.

In the meantime, Thomas Stransky, CSP, an American Paulist priest who had served in Rome, helping initiate the Vatican Secretariat for Christian Unity, had succeeded Landrum as rector, and would guide the institute for ten fruitful years, exploiting its location to involve intellectuals and activists from both sides of the "seam." Ten years in the Vatican Congregation for Christian Unity made him a natural for Tantur. Moreover, his decision to engage Vivi Siniora as "house matron" shaped the next decade more significantly than any other. Sensing the need for a woman's presence to help make this extensive house a home for its temporary residents, Tom invited a Danish woman who had married into the Siniora family of East Jerusalem to serve in that capacity at Tantur. Mother of four children, then in various stages of education in Jerusalem and the United States, Vivi was hesitant to take on such a large responsibility yet agreed to "give it a try." That was all Tantur needed, for her rare combination of intelligence and intuition quickly crafted a role that became indispensable. She had acquired colloquial Arabic during her stay with the Siniora family in East Jerusalem. Soon after completing her secondary education in Denmark, and meeting Benoit during a Holy Land pilgrimage, she followed her instinct to return to the Holy Land, with her father's blessing. His mother became her second mother; his family, her family. Combining a Danish ethos for order with a Palestinian sense of hospitality, Vivi elegantly accomplished what Tom had hoped for: the house became a home, as countless residents during that decade and more will testify.

At the end of 1997, Tantur was to celebrate twenty-five years of scholars and programs, so some of us who had served as rector were invited to participate. Our associate provost at Notre Dame at the time, Timothy Scully, CSC, had also mandated a review of overseas programs, so their director, Tom Bogenschild, asked if I would do an evaluation while I was there. I had long been made conscious of the way our student program had virtually neglected Israel in leaning towards Palestine, so agreed to evaluate the program, but with the help of a colleague, Alan Dowty, who had just completed a book on "the Jewish state" and who had noted the lacuna regarding Israel when teaching students returning from Jerusalem. We simply had to do it together; Tom agreed, so we did just that. The result impressed Tim Scully to the point where he saw "it could be our best international program," yet felt it would take a few years to "iron out," so asked me if I would be willing to devote myself to it for a period of five years: fall in Notre Dame, spring in Tantur. I was more than willing, as we shall see, yet what made our sketch of a program so appealing? The fact that we quickly saw that while previous programs had personally transformed students, their very structure prevented them from engaging with their peers, Israeli or Palestinian. So we betook ourselves to Hebrew University on one side, and Bethlehem on the other, asking the institutions if they would mount a course "in English for our students yet open to your students," recognizing we could not anticipate students coming with linguistic skills in Arabic or in Hebrew. They were thrilled to do so, so we had a program!

But there was a further dimension to this transaction, which I shared with our Associate Provost, Tim Scully, and with my confrere Monk Malloy, as president of Notre Dame, which assured me that the step was not undertaken for my advantage. *En route* to the twenty-fifth celebration of Tantur, I had participated in a symposium at the American University in Cairo (AUC), staying with my French Dominican community (of which more later) and connected with Bill and Therese Demars and their family from University Village, now resident in Cairo while Bill taught political science at AUC. The symposium topic—"exchange across the Mediterranean over the ages"—elegantly described my newfound field of inquiry. Cairo received me as an old friend, and as my favorite bus ride across the north Sinai brought me nearer Jerusalem, I felt more and more "at home." Arriving at Tantur, the lights of Bethlehem after supper made me realize I was indeed at home, as everything conspired to tell me. So much so that I knew I had to ask, in Ignatian fashion, what that meant, for it was truly overpowering—not something I had "thought up." So again following Ignatius, unable to consult God directly, I inquired of my friends in Jerusalem. Tom Stransky had recently announced that he had two more years as rector of Tantur. Was that what I was being called to do? I was not sure, but hesitation to "take up something again" gave me pause. Yet something compelling had overwhelmed me, so I crafted a letter to the president of Notre Dame, who should at least know where my heart was, freeing him to share it with whomever he saw fit.

Tim Scully had seen that letter, so in proposing a tenure of each spring for five years, noted that this should be preferable to the rectorship of Tantur, since it would permit me to spend half of each year at Notre Dame, rather than leaving for Jerusalem completely. I was immensely relieved, as he confirmed my suspicions about the rector's role not being my call at this time, but also because he offered me something I never could have asked for: the gift of following the impulse I had felt so profoundly, and doing so under university auspices with students who could palpably profit from the program Alan and I had sketched out in a moment of inspiration. Accepting Tim's proposal that evening in the fall of 1997 effectively launched the rest of my life.

It would be played out for nearly ten years, as events shaped our lives at Tantur, on the "seam" between Jerusalem and Bethlehem, Israel and Palestine. Four years after the celebrated handshake between Rabin and Arafat, Israeli intransigence had only built up frustration in what was to have become Palestine. Yet we brought our students, some fifteen each year, into that maelstrom, teaching them how to avoid specific intersections as they walked to Bethlehem University twice a week, and opening them to interaction with rabbinic students at a Jewish-Christian study center in West Jerusalem where three of us—a Jew, a Muslim, and a Christian—led a theology course. Once a week they went to Hebrew University for a lecture series on "the situation" by distinguished professors there, in a seminar setting with Israeli students. The plan Alan and I had sketched out was taking shape! Omar Othman, a resident of nearby Beit Safafa, whom Landrum Boling had dubbed "the best teacher I ever met," led them into colloquial Arabic, while the final course was the land itself. We traveled the Holy Land together, extending its reaches to include Jordan and Egypt, while demanding in the end a creative composition detailing—in an idiom personal to each—the import of all this! That program lasted for two years, culminating, as it turned out, in the Pope's visit to the Holy Land in the spring of 2000—a high point if there ever was one! I was satisfied that Tim had been right: this had to be Notre Dame's best international program! I had no experience of others, of course, nor do I relish ranking, but I knew ours was superb, and can now attest to its lasting effects on the students. Again, their single most powerful memory will doubtless be of Vivi, who even supplied them with peanut butter, after I had done my best to adapt them to humus as the "Middle East peanut butter."

So we had special reason for watching the debacle of Camp David II with dismay and consternation, and when Sharon did his "cakewalk" on the Haram ash-Sharif (Temple Mount) at the end of September that same year (2000), it did not take long to realize our program was doomed. We waited as long as we could to make our decision, but in the end made it before the university made it for us, in time for the students we had recruited to select courses for the spring semester. One African-American young woman found the School for International Training (SIT) and set out for Uganda, announcing "doors close, windows open," and her courageous step inspired me to help launch Notre Dame's current collaboration with SIT in Uganda. Since I was not listed for teaching in the spring, I managed to slip away to Tantur, for I knew how hard it would be for Michael McGarry, the relatively new rector, to find out he had signed on for a war! I knew I had to be there, with the same certitude that led me to cancel the program for students, once I sensed I could not assure their safety in what was bound to follow. I have always been grateful to the university for permitting me that freedom, trying in the years following when my presence at Tantur was extended by various institutional maneuvers, to express that gratitude in being present for the staff in every way I could, encouraging those who "hung in to keep the doors open," hoping for a better day. That better day has finally dawned, as the university gingerly took up a summer program, under the inspired leadership of Patrick Gaffney, to test the waters for a full-fledged program of a potency similar to the one we inaugurated and destiny gave us two years to execute.

Cairo

Cairo completes Jerusalem for me, as the two mentors mentioned introduced me to the inescapably philosophical dimensions of interfaith work—Marcel Dubois, OP, with Jews, and Georges Anawati, OP, with Muslims—to show how comparative work will always involve entering into diverse traditions so as to see how one can fertilize the other: "mutual illumination," my colleague Brad Malkovsky calls it. The twin Dominican venues in Jerusalem and Cairo opened to me a world of medieval exchange in philosophical theology, suggesting the shape of our task today. The hospitality of the Cairo community, with their superb library, resulted in two books, *Knowing the Unknowable God* (1986) and *Freedom and Creation in Three Traditions* (1993), later supplemented by translations of three major works of the "Islamic Augustine," al-Ghazali. The ever-receptive Cairo community of Dominicans also proved to be a crossroads where itinerant Islamicists came to know one another in an "institute" more home than institution. Lasting friendships with Tony Johns (Canberra) and his student Tony Street (Cambridge) were initiated there. The language was French while the reception was Egyptian, with a garden offering shade from Cairo summers and an unparalleled library. With that venue, Cairo became a third home. Indeed, the genius of IDEO (Institut Dominicain d'Etudes Orientales) lies in its capacity to initiate into the intellectual world of Islam scholars who come with three strikes against them: not being Muslim, never quite knowing the language (who but native Arabic speakers do?), and often quite unlettered in rich

Islamic commentary traditions. Located a few kilometers from al-Azhar's original center in the city of Cairo, and renowned for its long-standing "apostolate of friendship," inaugurated by Abouna Anawati and carried on in multiple ways by members of the community, the institute offers access to Egyptian counterparts who would otherwise be difficult to meet. Furthermore, in this process of acclimatization, a metaphor may occur to put one at ease with Cairo traffic, as it did with me: rather than streets crowded with cars, better see them as rivers filled with boats, to be ready as pedestrians to negotiate the fluid terrain like fish swimming upstream!

Once Cairo had become home to me, I returned to visit the community whenever I could. My confrere Patrick Gaffney felt the same way, so one day we converged serendipitously to celebrate the dedication of the imposing new library extension, brought to completion by Jean-Jacques Perrenès, OP, the Dominican prior called upon to forge a new life for the institute in the wake of Anawati's departure for the Kingdom at eighty-seven in 1994. Jean-Jacques had served with Timothy Radcliffe when that Oxford Dominican had been elected as Master, so was well acquainted with the Dominican order worldwide and in a position to draw younger confreres to study Islam in Cairo. He had also mastered English, so was able to welcome those from anglophone countries, as well as insert the institute into the scholarly world of Cairo, whose *lingua franca* had migrated from French to English. Jean-Jacques has recently completed the life of Abouna Anawati, after poring through writing projects half completed, as well as the mass of letters and conference brochures that had accumulated in his cluttered study, to present a rounded picture of this man of God and of all things human, whose presence animated the house as well as countless corners of Cairo and the world: *Georges Anawati: Un chrétien égyptien devant le mystère de l'Islam* (2008). (Frank Peters, whom I first met at the Dominican house, had dedicated his *Children of Abraham* to "Georges Anawati, of Cairo and the Kingdom of God.") His capacity for intellectual work and for friendship seemed inexhaustible, often absorbing him long into the night, yet each morning he would arise early to offer Mass with the Daughters of Charity next door.

The new library edifice, whose construction was facilitated by Jean-Jacques' reaching out to funding sources worldwide, was named "Bibliotèque Georges Chehata Anawati." The dedication day drew longtime friends of the institute from Egyptian intellectual circles, with Coptic and Catholic bishops as well as government ministers. But for Patrick and me, and for the community, the celebrated guest was Serge de Laugier de Beaurecueil, a Dominican who had begun his study of Islam in Cairo, then migrated to Kabul to follow the spiritual path of his master, Ansari (whose works he translated), only to fall in love with Afghan culture and serve its street children in ways detailed in a memoir, *Nous avons partagé le pain et le sel* ("We have shared bread and salt"). In his early nineties, he was the youngest person there! More recently, a young Dominican from Burkina Faso, Minlib Dallh, has successfully completed a dissertation (at Exeter) analyzing in penetrating detail the way Serge's immersion in the Afghan mystic Ansari effectively enriched his Dominican spirituality.

Subsequent visits to IDEO have always been renewing, if only to walk the corridors so filled with human warmth, where I was able (with his help) to execute the project Abouna Anawati had originally blessed. Most recently, we received Michael Fitzgerald, currently apostolic delegate to Egypt and the Arab League, who finds periodic refuge there, along with Cardinal Tauran from the Vatican. Having served with the Secretariat of State, Tauran was making casual comments on Israeli politics that I found ill-informed, so contradicted him, until his shocked expression reminded me, one does not challenge cardinals! Yet the community covered for me, as they had in other diplomatic gaffes over the years: one summer when Bernard Lewis came to pay homage to Abouna Anawati, I could not help taking issue with him as well. Yet the grace with which this international community receives even Americans gives testimony once again to the genius of the Catholic institution of religious communities: to belong to one is to be welcome in any other—an unparalleled gift. Moreover, what has ever impressed me with the Cairo Dominicans has been their abiding care for one another, doubtless enhanced by their international composition, and the fact that all have been displaced to make their home in Cairo.

Hania

On a more personal note celebrating the intellectual stimulus of the eastern Mediterranean, my peregrinations had restored a college friendship in the person of Nikos Stavroulakis (née Peter Stavis), whose itinerary had taken him from Notre Dame to graduate study at Michigan and Oxford, then on a roots journey to Athens and on to Jerusalem and Istanbul, only to return to Athens to found the Jewish Museum of Greece. In 1958, he had touched down in Rome en route to Athens for a brief visit at the airport while I was studying there, though we would not meet again until 1979 in Athens. Thenceforth I made an effort to see him on every trip to the Holy Land, and after he returned to his ancestral city of Hania in western Crete, to restore the synagogue there, our visits became annual. Our friendship is the richer for uniting opposites: I joined an institution while Nikos became one! His capacity for friendship is legendary; many who help sustain his unique interfaith work do so as a pledge of their faith in his vision and presence. Being an artist, architect, writer, and student of Greek Jewry makes him a natural consultant for museum projects, and his Ottoman predilection has recently led him to assist a fledgling Jewish museum in Salonika, where the Sephardic Jews from Andalusia were offered refuge by the Ottoman emperor, to flourish for more than four centuries until decimated by the Nazis. Certainly our friendship has catalyzed my transformation into the Mediterranean person I feel myself to have become.

That lifelong friendship is appropriately concretized and symbolized in the Etz Hayyim synagogue in Hania in Crete, which Nikos elegantly restored (with the help of the World Monuments Fund) and has continued to animate. Restored as "a memorial to the Cretan Jews who perished in 1944, . . . like the tent of Abraham, the synagogue has open doors and does not discriminate between those who wish to either visit or participate in its life" (Constitution for Etz Hayyim Synagogue). Many pilgrims have found their way to the door of this elegantly modest place of prayer, and on entering do just that—pray! Indeed, Etz Hayyim offers a model for spaces like this, usually found on the side streets of our parlous world, where hospitality exercises its countercultural valence in the face of the stereotyping endemic to corridors of power. They give silent yet eloquent witness to the way hospitality exercised within different sectors of our polarized world can open fresh possibilities in its wake. While optimism, with its twin sister, prediction, will prove to be "fool's gold," authentic hope can both fuel and result from such initiatives and the individuals whose tireless efforts have helped realize them. In these places we learn that *hope* is a "theological virtue"; that is, we cannot fabricate it ourselves, but it will be found by those who seek it.

Forging a Mediterranean Person in the Face of Islam

For a religious person, the perennial question remains: How is it that "religion" can so easily be co-opted by unscrupulous politicians to contribute to the shrill, self-righteous denigration of the other? How can a revelatory message be so easily reduced to "identity politics"? And of course, what are "religious leaders" doing about it? In fact, the phrase seems no more apt for them than for "political leaders," as both fall prey to interests that so easily trivialize their stated mandate, God-given in both cases! So the drama in the "Holy Land" is but an ongoing version of what we have seen in so many other parts of the world: the Balkans, the African Great Lakes region, Central Asia, South Asia, Indonesia, and other parts of West Asia. Several candidates compete to explain "what is really going on," but they all come under the name of human venality, which faith communities have proven virtually powerless to temper over the centuries. And less effective, it seems, the more such communities have tried to influence political power. Might that mean that any impact of faith communities rests in their powerlessness? The presence of the Mennonite-inspired Christian Peacemaker Team in the violent atmosphere of Hebron in Palestine offers such a testimony, and in time may simply erode pointless Israeli reliance on weapons as well as Jewish settlers' righteous claims to exclusive possession of their land. Theirs is a testimony of faith rather than a manifestation of religious identity, speaking eloquently to those with whom they come in daily contact.

Islam in Bosnia

More recently, the hospitality of a distinguished Muslim friend in Sarajevo, Rusmir Mahmutcehajic, introduced me to Bosnian Islam. Describable either as a "pocket" or a "crossroads," Islam in the Balkans enjoys Ottoman Sufi origins, with a history of daily interaction with Jews and Christians that can be mined especially today, after unscrupulous politicians were able to hijack those religious differences to pit neighbor against neighbor. Sarajevo bore the brunt of Serbian nationalist irredentism, shamelessly abetted by the established Orthodox Church, though deplored by some vocal monastic centers in Serbia. To experience Bosnia today, and do so through the eyes and heart of an activist scholar in love with all of its people, as Rusmir clearly is, reminds one of the promise of

Andalusia—despite the political fragility of a brokered set of accords. An Islam of this genre, at once popular and sophisticated, is bound to incur "excommunication" from Salafi groups (often funded from Saudi Arabia), especially because it offers a rich testimony to the pluralism present within Islam itself. And for that very reason it is to be cherished and made better known. When Anne-Marie Schimmel, the noted Harvard Islamic scholar, came to Sarajevo and entered Rusmir's *tekke* (Sufi mosque), she was overwhelmed: "I have searched all over South Asia for something like this, only to find it in my backyard." Indeed, one cannot but sense an enduring spiritual font in these forms of Islam, one that prompts Christians to a deeper appreciation of their own mystical sources.

We experienced this recently when 138 Muslim intellectuals and religious leaders issued "A Common Word between Us and You," to which the Vatican responded (in 2008) by initiating a Catholic-Muslim forum, jointly directed by a board of five respected members from each faith community. And what makes this so imperative today (as "A Common Word" insists) is the apparent paradox that our "information age" displays a pervasive penchant for clichés, allowing them to prevail in the game of demonizing "the other." Yet the paradox dissolves when we recall that *information* can so easily be packaged and bought by the highest bidder, so controlled in the interest of the powerful. So it appears that nothing can substitute for engaging in the living encounters these reflections detail. My own itinerary traces a topography meant to expose the panoply of personal encounters that have moved me to that engagement. Nor need we travel extensively for apertures like these to open; indeed, anyone awakened to the way stereotypes constrain us will welcome an opportunity to meet "someone different." If the desperate situation of Bosnia awakened me to persons who offered heartening resources in the midst of Sarajevo, years in Israel/Palestine similarly affected me: enraged at injustices continually perpetrated yet seldom rising to the level of "information" for prevailing media, I was also moved to a new level of hope, as victims of that very injustice display dignity and endurance in the face of overwhelming power. Yet we must meet the people themselves to dissolve the stereotypes offered of them as we discover the sources of their inner strength. One finds just that in participants in the "Parents' Circle," who have learned how to share grieving among persons from both Israeli and Palestinian society. If their tragedies were caused by "the other side," their response offers a paradigm for what Sarah McMillen, a young friend who has tasted deeply of the "Parents' Circle," calls "hospitality to difference." That could well be the epitaph for the journey given to me to take.

7

Apple Farm, Loretto Motherhouse, and Gender Complementarity

Apple Farm (Three Rivers, Michigan)

ALTHOUGH APPLE FARM IS located but an hour's drive from South Bend, where I spent forty-two years teaching at the University of Notre Dame, as a spiritual *locus* it rather lies at the confluence of exotic places. These I have already described as my intellectual and spiritual homes. Illuminated by the signal presence of Helen Luke for thirty years, and animated by a sustaining community, Apple Farm has offered spiritual sustenance to seekers for nearly half a century.

Holy Cross requires its members to undertake an annual retreat, as well as advising that each find a "spiritual director," in the tradition of Ignatius of Loyola. "Spiritual friendship," embodied by monastic communities from their beginning, is also highly valued in active congregations such as Holy Cross. It was my closest friend in our congregation, John Gerber, who brought Apple Farm to my attention. He himself had been directed to seek out Helen Luke in her capacity as a Jungian analyst by friends in other places. Her analytic skills were hardly inconsiderable, but what Helen became for each of us was, in fact, a spiritual director. No doubt her training in Jungian analysis helped her circumvent our endemic self-deceptions in matters spiritual, but it was Helen's personal charism that made her so deft at spiritual direction. Her personal gifts truly developed in the context of a community that gathered around her. Helen Luke became, to be sure, that community's guiding light and nurturing source. In fact, my own bimonthly visits to Apple Farm inevitably pulled me out of the complexities of a university world into a quasi-monastic setting. Apple Farm's simplicity did half the work of removing my blinders so as to listen to Helen. With dreams as the medium, her strategy helped release me from philosophical discourse into the play of imagination.

The intellectual vein into which I tapped at Apple Farm finds resonance in Islam. There prophets are deemed superior to scholars precisely in their ability to suffuse understanding with imagination—in order to be intelligible to all human beings. This special virtue is found paradigmatically in "the Prophet," of course; however, it also characterizes the language of the "inimitable Qur'an." Yet nothing seems more elusive to modern Western minds than "the imagination." And if poets dwell in it, for that very reason will they refuse to articulate imagination prosaically.

So insofar as I possessed a Western philosophical mind, I needed the guidance of Helen Luke, a master, and the context of an alternative community, Apple Farm. These were required if I were even to begin appreciating how true understanding will involve imagination as well as intellect. Coming to value imagination involved developing a resonance with dreams. My dreams, recorded in my journal, would later be illuminated in conversation with Helen. This regular practice, over twenty-five years, combined with Ignatius' daily discipline of using imagination to locate ourselves within the Scriptures, was deepened annually by a directed retreat. Eight days allowed these images time to enter the space of my own soul. Often accompanied by my Holy Cross sister friend, Elena Malits, John Gerber and I took to making our retreat over Christmas break with the Sisters of Loretto (in Kentucky near the Abbey of Gethsemani). Astute directors at Loretto could move each of us in directions suggested by our encounters with Helen Luke.

Loretto Motherhouse (Nerinx, Kentucky)

In the sixties I had begun to make retreats at the Abbey of Gethsemani in Kentucky when Thomas Merton was living there. I had relished the silence and quiet beauty of the topography of Nelson County, Kentucky, since retreats there during student days a decade earlier. I soon came to

feel, ironically, that the stately way in which the monastery was constituted militated against my own retreat, for I would be distracted the first
few days by wondering whether I should not become a monk. But any of
my friends could have told me I would make a lousy monk! So with John
Gerber, I sought another venue, and we settled upon the first week of
the calendar year, following Christmas week, seeking a climate less harsh
than northern Indiana with someone to direct our retreat. After a few
tries, we found the ideal person in Elaine Prevallet, a sister of Loretto,
who had become close to Helen Luke.

No distraction for me at the Loretto sisters' motherhouse, yet the
same gentle topography as Gethsemani. It proved natural to bring Elena Malits with us as well, since she had completed her dissertation on
Thomas Merton at Loretto, and was at home with that community. In
time, John and I also came to be at home in the Loretto community, so we
continued making our retreat there even after Elaine herself moved west
to Santa Fe. And after John's death in 1995, Elena and I kept on making
our annual retreat there, finding a superb director in Mary Fran Lottes.
The Loretto motherhouse has always held a singular attraction for me,
since it occupies the farm of Theodore Badin, the first priest ordained in
the United Sates—a circuit rider from the Ohio River to Lake Michigan.
He was the one who had offered the property with two lakes (that became
Notre Dame) to Edward Sorin, CSC, in the mid-nineteenth century. So
for Elena and me going to Loretto became a bit like returning to our Holy
Cross roots in this country, and we were delighted more recently to resume working with Elaine Prevallet when she returned to Loretto.

Gender Complementarity

If this scenario sounds quite feminine, it is indeed so, just as the complementarity between intellect and imagination already signals. My spiritual
journey clearly embodies a gender complementarity—with none of the
role-conventional overtones of that term. Indeed, Jung has taught me
how analogous the terms "masculine" and "feminine" can be, each illuminating the inner depths of both men and women.

Without this ongoing dream-discipline I am quite sure that I could
never have appreciated William Chittick's prescient exposition of the way
Ibn 'Arabi, the Muslim philosophical theologian and mystic, articulates

his views in language addressed to imagination as well as intellect. Understanding, indeed, for Ibn 'Arabi will inevitably involve both. This strong feminine infusion, in fact, brought me to a proper comprehension of interiority. As John of the Cross intimates throughout his work, the soul's relation to God is archetypally feminine—that is, receptive. Thus I am able to discover a strict continuity, extended in time, between that special summer in the Südtirol, Apple Farm, and Loretto. These constitute three precious locales whose magic works to open mind and heart to matters of the spirit. And each in its own way provided a counterpoint to the intense intellectual environments of Gregorian University and Notre Dame. Much as gender complementarity can contribute to interior awakening, so contrast of locales can open our spirit to dimensions unsuspected by academic worlds.

Helen Malits and I had met in the context of the University of Notre Dame and Saint Mary's College while we were both undergraduates in the early fifties. What brought us together was the "Young Christian Students" group already mentioned, imported from Europe on the cusp of the Second World War by Louis Putz, who had entered Holy Cross from Bavaria. He had emigrated to America in the 1920s to undertake high school and college studies, before being sent to France to help reseed the Congregation of Holy Cross in its ancestral home in the city of LeMans in the Sartre. His theological formation in LeMans and later in Paris coincided with the onset of the fruitful *nouvelle théologie* movement, whose "return to the sources" would eventually animate the documents of the Vatican Council II. At Notre Dame and Saint Mary's, Father Putz encouraged us in YCS to engage in social analysis in the living context of gospel reflection. This enabled us to live the practical consequences of our religious faith, shaped by the story of Jesus. Appealing to inquisitive minds fascinated with the dynamics of social change, YCS groups offered a way for young people to integrate faith with reason, and have fun doing so.

In this context I was attracted to Helen Malits' personal and intellectual vivacity, as we became coworkers and good friends. In the heady last days of my final year at Notre Dame, as her sophomore year was drawing to a close, I invited her to the gala to end the year (the "senior prom"), only to break the news that I felt impelled to cast my lot with the Congregation of Holy Cross at the end of the summer. She was less surprised by this than I had anticipated, though I had been slower than she to realize how intimately our lives were coming together. So those last weeks together were indeed bittersweet, as we enjoyed outings with friends at Lake Michigan and celebrated our growing intimacy. I found myself telling Elena that I loved her, somewhat to my own surprise, though she responded easily and confidently. Not until returning home and sharing all this with my sister did the potency of those final weeks break through to me.

Elena spent the following academic year studying in Europe with a peripatetic group that appealed to her sense of adventure. In her senior year at Saint Mary's we met briefly at Notre Dame during a YCS conference where she was scheduled to speak and I was attending as a seminarian. We bumped into each other in the hall, each trying to conceal nervousness. Then after graduating from Saint Mary's in 1956, she entered the novitiate of the Sisters of the Holy Cross on the western perimeter of the college campus. I had by then completed our novitiate, and after a year studying languages and philosophy at Notre Dame, was heading for Rome. Our next encounter would be her final profession as Sister Elena in the summer of 1962. I had just returned from Rome, and in the company of our friend and mentor, Louis Putz, attended Elena's final profession of vows.

While we had been separated by continents, our lives had already touched in an indelible way. It would take a concatenation of circumstances to restore the original connection between Helen-Elena and me in an ongoing and fruitful way. Louis Putz's counsel would prove invaluable when we began to negotiate a new relationship in line with our religious vows. Elena was teaching at Cardinal Cushing College in Boston, but came to Saint Mary's each summer to teach theology in the novitiate. So it was possible for us to do things together now and then, and again Louis Putz's presence proved most helpful, as did the guidance of Elena's good friend Sr. Charles Borromeo. There was also the sage advice of Tom Barrosse, who served as my superior-general, and with whom I would later teach in the National Major Seminary in Dhaka, Bangladesh. At a time (by now, the sixties and seventies) when countless priests, brothers, and sisters were leaving their religious orders to marry, Elena and I each needed elders among our Holy Cross community to help us share our lives within the family of Holy Cross.

Serendipitously, we both found such elder companions in our respective religious communities. Helen Luke, moreover, would serve each of us as a spiritual guide to accompany us on this journey. Tom Barrosse's advice about friendship between men and women in vows was succinct and to the point. Addressing this issues in a circular letter, he insisted: be honest with your spiritual director, and let your relations with one another be inclusive of others, rather than exclusive. Following Tom Barrosse's advice has allowed our respective local communities, as well as our families, to partake in our love, as Elena and I embarked on a path with a few, but not many precedents. (As Dierdre Carabine, an Irish philosopher and educator in Uganda, has adroitly put it: this is a path along which "men and women can express affection and friendship" without concomitant suspicion). Acceptance from our respective communities has been key to helping that to happen to each of us.

On September 15, 1973, Elena and I entered into what we call "our Covenant." Reading from the book of Deuteronomy that summer in the Office of Readings led to protracted discussions, so the patronal feasts of Holy Cross on September 14 and 15 appeared to be the right time to take some appropriate action. We met in the Log Chapel at Notre Dame, and our simple ceremony was witnessed by Fr. Putz and one of Elena's sisters. We read aloud our affirmations of what we would do and would not do to keep our relationship alive in Holy Cross. This Covenant provided a bellwether for assessing our fidelity to a very special relationship. From that day until the present Elena and I have experienced continual struggles, occasional failures, but most of all great joy.

My love for Elena allowed me to develop close friendships with many other Holy Cross sisters. And my own sister Nina's move to South Bend, after a divorce terminating twenty-seven years of marriage with seven children, led me even further into appreciating the world from a feminine perspective. Through her I tasted the emotional and financial travails of a woman in the wake of a divorce that a compounded set of circumstances had made inevitable. For fifteen years, we celebrated mass with supper together each Tuesday evening at her modest yet lovely home overlooking the St. Joseph River. In time, she was justly granted an annulment by the Catholic Church, which—as time and circumstance allowed—led her to a life together with the widower of a colleague with whom Nina had worked in the library at Satin Mary's College. Dick Klee's wife Lee had died unexpectedly of pancreatic complications, and her intuition that the complications could be fatal led to their union by a circuitous path. Providential, really, as Dick proved to be the husband Nina had always wanted. At their wedding, he passed me a discreet note that read, "It's Tuesday's at our house!"

Our resolve to share liturgy and supper weekly during those years contributed mightily to my education and sensitivity in such matters. Yet without Helen Luke's sage guidance, I would never have been able to appreciate what was happening in my life, especially the way my male perspectives were being stretched to include the feminine. This expansion was taking place not abstractly but personally, through these women so integral to my life.

In this way, expressions like "gender complementarity" came to life for me, rendering my vision of all things increasingly stereoscopic, both male and female. Perhaps the greatest gift from Elena's community has been our ability to travel together, always to destinations that included others, so we share a rich panoply of mutual friends. Opportunities for travel began with our joint participation in a group that has continued a fellowship forged out of the largesse of the Danforth Foundation, funding fellowships for graduate study to those who regarded "teaching as a Christian vocation." Extending the Danforth program to include the Kent Fellowship for similarly minded people in graduate studies, this rather evangelical foundation found itself funding Catholics as well. I was advised of this possibility by my friend Joe Cunneen, one of the founding editors of *Cross Currents*, during my initial year in philosophy at Yale, when I was selected for a Kent Fellowship on the cusp of my second year of studies. The continuing group—renamed the Society for Values in Higher Education—managed to meet annually every summer at a college campus with recreational facilities for a family-centered gathering. So the tone has always been richer than that of "professional meetings," offering an interdisciplinary fare that invariably enriched the following year's teaching. In fact, the major benefit of the annual fellows' conference was the way it has fostered nourishing friendships.

Our joint participation in these annual gatherings reinforced Tom Barrosse's advice regarding the shape of our friendship. More extensive travel began with my appointment as rector of the Tantur Ecumenical Institute in Jerusalem in 1980, which gave Elena the chance to bring her mother to the Holy Land, allowing us to participate in field trips in the now-conflicted land where Jesus lived. Later visits to Hania in Crete brought us into relatively frequent contact with Nikos Stavroulakis, whom we had both known in our undergraduate days as Peter Stavis, from Fond du Lac, Wisconsin. She was especially taken with the beauty of Hania harbor and Nikos' charming seventeenth-century Venetian home overlooking it.

Eventually, as decades of diabetes finally indicated overseas travel to be inadvisable, Elena would miss Hania above all, nor would she be able to fulfill her long-standing desire to taste Andalusia, as I have been able to do. Yet even in the face of her health restrictions, we have been able in recent years to enjoy the reunion of my eldest brother's family, relatives, and friends on a North Carolina beach. We were often able to combine that vacation with the annual Society for Values gathering, taking pleasure in the abundant time for conversation that travel by car affords.

The onset of arthritis in more recent years has proved more debilitating to Elena than more than five decades of type 1 diabetes. Yet the manner in which she has suffered these diminishments has given me and others a profound witness of transformation in a person not always known for her patience! ("Suffer" better expresses the situation than the American idiom "handle," which keeps everything at arm's length, when nothing is more intimate than our body's breakdowns.) Finally, our long-standing relationship of nearly sixty years has served to introduce me into the rich field of "gender difference" through the mysteries of a human love enfolded in our religious vows. It has also revealed my own disposition to dominate, which Elena's formidable assistance has somewhat helped to temper. Unveiling that propensity can only augur a great deal of unfinished business for me. It also makes me grateful, nonetheless, for the varied conflicts Elena and I have suffered through the years!

Epilogue

Fostering Trust in God (Tawakkul) through Islam and in East Africa

THE STORY GOES ON, of course, notably in the way our lives are enmeshed with our times. The cascade of events ending seventy years of Soviet experiments with state Marxism elicited a euphoria that quickly evaporated as ethnic conflicts unraveled for twenty subsequent years, often issuing in genocide: Sudan, Ethiopia/Eritrea, the Balkans, Rwanda/eastern Congo, Darfur, Iraq, and Afghanistan. I was privileged to spend much of that time in West Asia, and now in East Africa. Privileged, because one cannot escape experiencing the pain and fallout from such conflicts on site, even when not directly involved, as proximity removes many of the baffle plates inhibiting awareness of what is actually going on. The richness of individual lives animated by the grace of the Spirit can be overwhelming. In the last quarter century, as my intellectual and spiritual quest brought me in closer conjunction with Islam, the inclusive ways of that Spirit have also become palpable. Living in countries with a daily "call to prayer," as well as an annual celebration of Ramadan, has reminded me forcibly of our need for daily disciplines of prayer. As an African Catholic priest put it, in the face of often mindless criticism of Islam and Muslims, "Don't knock them; they have been getting me up to pray for years!" I feel the same way, as my Muslim friends remind me to say, "Alhamdulillah!"— "Praise be to God!"—in the midst of anger or dismay at the omnipresence of violence of all kinds in our world, much of it fomented by my own country. Indeed, my own spiritual life has been shaped by Muslim seekers, notably al-Ghazali (whom I have translated), Ibn 'Arabi (a Muslim counterpart to Meister Eckhart), as well as by contemporary friends in the Holy Land and in South Asia.

Retrospective:
How a Christian Can Come to Appreciate Islam

The model here is Louis Massignon, whose life introduced so many to interfaith understanding and spiritual companionship in the first half of the twentieth century. In France an entire society is devoted to his work, and Mary Louise Gude, CSC, who composed his biography in English (*Louis Massignon: The Crucible of Compassion* [1966]), came to know its principal members. She and I organized a conference on his work at Notre Dame in the nineties, revealing a special cadre of people, notably Sidney Griffiths, attracted to his theo-poetic way of relating our two faiths. A close friend of Paul VI, Massignon's reflections on Islam helped shape the landmark Vatican II document on Christianity and other faiths, *Nostra Aetate*. His singular witness was initially continued through Dominicans in Cairo and White Fathers in Tunis and Rome, so Catholic interfaith encounters with Islam tend to be francophone, while Protestant pioneers were anglophone, inspired by Duncan MacDonald, a Presbyterian who served in Lebanon at the American University in Beirut and later inspired a Christian-Muslim center at Hartford Seminary in Connecticut.

My growing appreciation of Islam has been through Muslims—persons enter into dialogue; religions don't—beginning with the 1975 summer at Tantur, extending though initial encounters in East Bengal, and growing appreciably once my center of gravity shifted to Jerusalem and Cairo. I have found that Muslims bring a palpable sense of the presence of God to our exchange, nurtured in hospitality. Everyone who has spent time in a Muslim society remarks on the ever-present hospitality; Louis Massignon sees it as a continual reminder to Christians of the two commandments into which Jesus condensed "the law and the prophets." The gentleness displayed by my friend Mustafa Abu-Sway (which he tells us is traditionally enjoined upon Muslim men) stands in stark contrast to the stereotype cultivated by extremists and perpetrated by Western media. Muslim friends have taught me how to live and to pray in a way that helps me follow the path Jesus invites us to walk with him. No alienation here; rather a sense of homecoming. Nor is there any dilution of the distinctive mark of Christian faith: that our revelation is in a person, not a book—a stark reminder to some evangelical Christians (whom I dub "Muslim Christians") of the fact that rather than coming to bring us God's word in the New Testament (as the Muslim accolade of "people of the book" might imply), Jesus *is* God's Word incarnate. Appreciating the appeal of Islam stems as much from the differences as from similarities with Christian faith.

An encounter with three African-American women directing the Muslim community in Jackson, Mississippi, taught me as much. Initiating our meeting with the parallel formulas: "We believe that Jesus is the Word of God made human, while you believe the Qur'an to be the word of God made book," we proceeded to come to such rich mutual understanding that one of them suddenly queried, "If you know so much about Islam, why are you not a Muslim?" I had met that question before, appreciating the love it shows for their faith, so had a ready response. I recalled the parallel formulas with which we began—a ploy designed to emphasize the affinities between Jesus and the Qur'an as well as deflect standard comparisons of Qur'an and Bible, which lead nowhere—interjecting the coy response: you cannot hug a book! One of them responded instantly: "We prefer our God not gendered, thank you!" *Touché!* Indeed, many revisionary attempts of Christian feminist theologians founder on the simple fact that being made flesh cannot help bringing gender with it! How much we can learn by comparing formulas that articulate both proximity and difference between Christianity and Islam! So it will always be; comparisons can only be by analogies, not identities. *Vive la différence!*

Yet there are as many incarnations of "Islam" as there are of "Christianity." I have so far experienced six distinct Islamic cultures: South Asian, West Asian, Egyptian, Iranian, Bosnian, and East African. My intellectual inquiry (in Arabic) has led me into Sunni tradition in al-Ghazali, and Shi'a tradition in Mulla Sadra, while the venues for that study continue to open me to distinct cultures through personal relations. Each has exhibited an overwhelming hospitality, the most striking being Iran. Shi'a fascination for philosophy instantly captivated me. Our introduction to a leading *mullah* in Qom, late at night in a shrine aglitter with lights reflected by cut glass chandeliers and filled with pilgrims, opened with tea and a query addressed to me: "Can we prove free creation of the universe from reason?" Startled, I recovered by replying: "No, because it is free." That did it; we were launched in a conversation as philosophical as it was religious.

That is Iran. After translating portions of Mulla Sadra's *magnum opus* on existence, tracing its emanating from the One only to return to the One via the response of human beings, I find Seyyed Hossain Nasr's contention convincing: that Islamic philosophy found new life as it returned to the heartland from Andalusia, in Suhrawardi, Ibn 'Arabi, and Mulla Sadra. In this second phase, Islamic philosophy becomes philosophical theology, accentuating the ineffable relation of creator to creatures in a fruitful dialectic between revelation and reason. This is hardly the place to rehearse all that, but it can remind us how crucial Iran becomes to this intellectual transition, promising to unveil spiritual implications as well.

The most recent impetus to interfaith encounter between Muslims and Christians, however, took place in Regensburg in 2006, when Josef Ratzinger addressed his colleagues as professor emeritus, offering an erudite summary of Christian tradition with a sidelong glance at Islam, intending to detail how faith communities need to employ the resources of reason to mine their revelatory tradition. Yet the sidelong glance proved to be a glancing blow, as he cited a former colleague's study of the last Byzantine emperor, replete with highly unflattering comments on Islam and the Prophet. Yet once the citation was imbedded in the spoken text, the media found it easy to attribute the unflattering remarks to the Pope himself, spurring riots on "the Muslim street." (I like to call it the day Professor Ratzinger became Pope, no longer free to engage in simple academic discourse. Yet the specific inclusion was injudicious as well; were one his tutor, one would have said: delete that example, it is bound to muddle your message. Which of course it did.) Yet the gaffe proved to be a *felix culpa*, eliciting a response from thirty-eight distinguished Muslim scholars within a month. They respectfully detailed Islam's long and fruitful engagement with reason, especially in the medieval period, and reminded him that the scholar he had cited to the contrary, Ibn Hazm of Cordova, in fact constituted a notable exception to this pattern.

Yet more than proper instruction was needed, nor is the Vatican used to being so instructed, so it befell a knowledgable intellectual, Prince Ghazi bin Muhammad bin Talal of Jordan, director of the Al-Bayt Institute in Amman, to take the initiative. Exercising considerable diplomatic skill, he enlisted wide endorsement throughout the variegated Muslim world of a document designed to show how Christianity and Islam must work together if the world is to have peace. Titled "A Common Word," it shows how they can do so since both faiths focus on love of God and love of neighbor. This landmark statement appeared a year after Regensburg, offering a telling response to queries regarding where Islam stands with respect to peacemaking in an increasingly violent world. (Responses of religious communities across the globe can be monitored on the Web site, acommonword.com). The significance of this action emerges when we consider how the absence of a single authoritative voice puts Islam at a singular disadvantage in our media-saturated world. What had over history fostered a rich pluralism has come to cripple the Muslim community today: "When will they renounce suicide bombing?" people ask, even though every Imam I know regularly does so. Yet the major media need a common voice, which Prince Ghazi proved able to elicit. The number of Muslim signatories has mushroomed, as have symposia and media events responding to this document.

In fact, the cross-current of exchange between Muslim and Christian communities in the period since the Regensburg address dwarfs anything that happened in the fourteen centuries previous. So one cannot but infer that something significant is taking place in the teeth of European Islamophobia and predictable American xenophobia against Muslims after the 2001 al-Qaeda strategic attack. If we take this opening together with popular uprisings against long-standing, unresponsive political regimes, initiated in Tunisia and Egypt and soon spreading to the wider Arab world, we have to recognize how Islam can be a constructive force in our parlous world. I can only be grateful to the inspiration that moved me to become involved thirty years ago, only to mark out a clear vocation today. The fruits of this long-term involvement with Jews, Christians, and Muslims has been published by Blackwell as *Towards a Jewish, Christian, Muslim Theology* (2011), for Christians cannot begin to speak without acknowledging Jesus' insistence that "salvation is from the Jews" (John 4:22). So while "A Common Word" focused on the need for bilateral understanding, the document itself necessarily has recourse to Hebrew Scriptures to make its point of commonality. Moreover, it is extraordinary to find thirty years of scholarship and engagement come to so fine a focus. And a focus brought exquisitely to light by a newfound filmmaker friend, Jacob Bender, whose historical documentary *Out of Cordoba* shows how we could find our future behind us with more faith and trust in the one God whom Jews, Christians, and Muslims worship.

A Fresh Life in East Africa with Holy Cross

Now East Africa continues the story in a new key. Arriving here to serve my Holy Cross religious community, some of my confreres wondered at my concern for Islam. Uganda hardly represents an ecumenical climate, as the British colonial administration promoted an Anglican clone, the "Church of Uganda" to counterbalance Catholic missionaries from France. Subsequent colonial history stirred a sociopolitical split between Catholics and Protestants (as this Anglican clone is decidedly Protestant), leading at independence to political parties separated by religious affiliation. The result is little or no conversation between Christians, and even less formal exchange with Muslims. Nor is there much animosity either; Christians and Muslims share work space easily, and we find a number of mixed families as well. Yet ignorance can often foment the inevitable stereotypes, even when living quite close to one another. When one of my confreres stated, "You cannot talk with Muslims," and proceeded to insist on this categorical statement though it was easily falsified with one encounter, I did just that, informing him the next morning that I had just spoken with Muslim friends in Gaza! Moreover, in the East African context, tribal differences can be far more volatile, so interfaith animosity is less evident, though my friends tell me it can emerge acutely at funerals. Similar things can be said for "mixed societies" in the Arab world as well, where these two religious groups have lived together for centuries, as William Dalrymple details for West Asia in *From the Holy Mountain*. Often the touted exception, Lebanon, a country that prides itself on its interfaith mosaic, is interlaced with animosities that will not die. As I write this, the nearby mosque in Kampala enjoins us to celebrate Ramadan, with especially haunting Qur'anic chants from early morning—another plus to living in a world with Muslim neighbors, whose patterns remind us to pray as well.

The invitation of our provincial superior to assist our Holy Cross District of East Africa brought me in 2007 to Uganda, to our Holy Cross community house in Kampala and to Uganda Martyrs University. Uganda's warm and welcoming people instantly convey a distinct feeling of being at home. Moreover, passing the three-quarter century mark better inclines me to learn what Uganda has to teach us: patience! The most telling example: for the first encounter of the day, one simply cannot begin with business, but one must first ask how the other is: how did you sleep? A simple recognition that we are engaged with a person, but one so easily forgotten in the West. My brief has been to utilize a teaching post at Uganda Martyrs University to explore ways our Holy Cross community could be present there. A relatively new venture of Ugandan laymen sponsored by the Uganda bishops' conference, UMU (as it is called) began in 1993, inspired by a dynamic duo: a Belgian "White Father" with extensive experience in Uganda, Michel Lejeune, and Dierdre Carabine, an Irish philosopher with singular organizational ability. My initial visit to UMU was an exploratory one, encouraged by David Tyson, the Indiana province provincial who had proposed the move, so that the decision would more properly be mine. With Tom McDermott, an outstanding confrere who had spent his entire priestly life in East Africa, we mounted the hill from Lake Victoria to the sylvan beauty of the UMU campus, and I was reminded of what Notre Dame must have been like 140 years before. With Dee Carabine, an accomplished cellist, playing the guitar at mass, it seemed that everyone did a little of everything. Michel Lejeune not only displayed a command of things, but clearly took time to speak with staff, inquiring into their well-being. In short, UMU was a family enterprise, and that so moved me that I signed on immediately.

In a short fifteen years, it has become what they dreamed: a university that focuses on teaching, to model for students the kinds of values that East Africa (and the world!) needs. Its location on an historic mission station overlooking Lake Victoria, eighty kilometers south of the capital, Kampala, fosters a vital synergy between students and faculty. Departments are largely practical in nature—education, business, health, building, and architecture—surrounding a core Institute of Ethics and Development. The current vice-chancellor (president), Charles Olweny, invited my confrere Claude Pomerleau, CSC, to spearhead a Faculty of Diplomacy and International Relations, drawing on his extensive experience in Chile. For myself, teaching Catholic social teaching and political Islam, which my students soon realized should be called "Muslim social teaching," made me acutely aware of fruitful crossovers, which I suspect stem at root from each being grounded in a universe freely created. Although Muslims in the class were few, small beachheads in interfaith relations proved possible. Beyond teaching, I came to treasure colleagues in Ethics and Development. Max Ngabirano published his Leuven dissertation to show the way disparate narratives can reveal the lineaments of conflict endemic to the Great Lakes region of Africa, comprising Uganda,

Burundi, Rwanda, and the Democratic Republic of Congo (DRC). My office-mate, Margaret Angucia, published the results of her doctoral work at Groningen (in Holland) in an arresting compilation and analysis of the stories of children abducted by the Lord's Resistance Army in their brutal incursions into Acholiland in northern Uganda: *Broken Citizenship* (2010). Peter Kanyandago, who has taught and held diverse offices at UMU from its inception, can bring a staunchly African critical edge to any discussion.

So when I was asked to work up a comprehensive curriculum for philosophy and religious studies for the university, I proceeded to incorporate a critical postcolonial perspective into each course, rather than spice a Western syllabus with a random course in "African philosophy." Providentially, a longtime colleague and friend from Wooster College, Richard Bell, also a penetrating student of Simone Weil, whose study of "restorative justice" effectively initiated a fresh approach to the subject, crafted a fine critical African approach in his *Understanding African Philosophy* (2002). After assimilating an African voice, he showed how that could be used to puncture smug Western presumptions of superiority which can easily extend to philosophy as well. The students whom I have come to know and respect include a Muslim young woman from Kenya, a Congolese young man who had first to master English before he could serve as student body president, and a Ugandan who has introduced a vigorous student program in human and civil rights. The last two were rewarded (yet severely tested) in being invited to a student-faculty symposium at the Kroc Institue for International Peace Studies at Notre Dame in the depth of winter 2011.

The surroundings of Uganda Martyrs University, overlooking Lake Victoria, can be breathtaking. Sitting on a bench in a refreshing breeze, I am overwhelmed by the way the people of Uganda, young and old, have received me. It takes me back thirty years, to the end of the Ignatian retreat of thirty days, hearing Jesus say (John 15:15) that he wanted me, engaged in serving him all these years, to be his friend. And if anything can show me how to make that crucial shift, it will be the people among whom I am privileged to live and work, who cultivate friendships spontaneously. In their reception, grace becomes tangible, as it especially has for me in coming to know Josephine Adubango and David Tshimba.

As both her parents succumbed to HIV/Aids, Josephine was orphaned at twelve with a brother *seven years* younger. Finding themselves without a home on the streets of Kampala, she was providentially directed to an orphanage, which she persuaded to take her brother as well. Excelling there, she won a scholarship to UMU, where she earned her brother's school fees by assisting students from French-speaking Burundi to compose in English. Her brother, Chan, multitalented in music and dance, has gone on to direct creative productions for the renowned Taibah School in Uganda. After volunteering with the Nebbi district local government in her home region of West Nile, Josephine put her education in Ethics and Development to distinctive use with the Agha Khan foundation, who soon engaged her to become their communications officer for Uganda under the East Africa Quality in Early Learning (EAQEL) project. Her elder sister, Immy (Imelda), a single parent of four, while less fortunate in the wake of their parents' death, is as valiant a woman as is Josey, and it has been a privilege to know her spirited family. Stories like theirs can only animate us to give thanks to a God who directs our lives so palpably, and to those like Josephine who have responded so gratefully to opportunities granted.

David Tshimba came to UMU from Goma and eastern Congo, so had to work on his English from the outset. That hardly inhibited him from coming to know many people, as his acquaintance with my confrere, Claude Pomerleau, began on a bench as they were talking. When he answered his mobile phone in French, that initiated their relationship, since Claude's family language was originally French. David was elected to chair the student council, but that did not distract him from pursing a deeper understanding of the conflict that has inundated his Kivu region of Congo. I came to meet his mother and father, and responded to an invitation to visit them in Goma, traveling by bus through Rwanda. It is hard to imagine a more strikingly beautiful country, so one's heart can only bleed in imagining the horrors of so recent a genocide. Goma is graced, one might say, with a volcano in the middle of the city, one that erupted in January 2002, inundating their home with ash, and separating mother from children for three days. They were reunited on a terrain that their father had providentially purchased long before, living in tents while their lovely home was being built. Their father, passionate about education, drove a petrol lorry from Mombasa to Goma for years, to educate the seven children, while their mother, an accountant, took a further degree in Scripture at the local university to be able to teach catechism in the parish, as well as a master's degree in health and community development in order to become an accomplished social agent for change in the badly affected local communities. While we were in Goma, we visited a UNDP camp filled with children, with a gracious and competent Charlotte keeping things in order. I learned never to visit a camp with children without taking scores of BIC pens; in their eagerness to learn, everyone wants one. One of the joys of teaching young people is meeting their families, and we can only stand in awe at the way faith can nourish a loving family life in the midst of threatening insecurity.

Blessedly, these relationships, which have blossomed into friendships, can fairly summarize four years of teaching at UMU. The size of the campus (twelve hundred residents), together with its relative isolation (eighty-four kilometers south of Kampala astride the equator), fosters interaction between faculty and students. Once I was able to spend the middle part of each week on campus; sharing the house of the Brothers of Christian Instruction convinced me that a Holy Cross presence here would require a residence where both staff and students could live and interact. Yet after dedicating four years to teaching and interacting with the community to that end, it also became clear that our East African district was not yet ready to undertake such a work, though I am convinced that we shall do so before long. Africa slowly teaches us that such ventures take time: a seed has been planted for others to water if they so wish. In the meantime, however, marvelous friends among colleagues and students offer a harbinger of how we might implant in East Africa the peculiar educational quality that characterizes Holy Cross in North and South America as well as the Asian subcontinent: living with our students so as to help them realize their potential, growing ourselves in the process. My experience inspires me to hope that Holy Cross will find its way to a house and a presence there before long, to extend our East African commitment to higher education to lay students as well. Forty-two years at Notre Dame have already detailed how that ineluctable process can shape those involved in it, forging lifelong friendships.

Holy Cross in East Africa

It has been a joy to serve our international Holy Cross community and to taste the ways in which a religious family of men and women, as brothers and sisters to one another, can be a propitious vehicle for intercultural exchange in the larger Christian world. East Africa has confirmed my initial experience of the advantages specific to Holy Cross as an international family, first noted in Bangladesh in 1975. The intervening thirty-plus years, taking me to West Asia and North Africa, expanded and enriched the initial experience of South Asia, now finding expression in East Africa. So all is gift, especially the surprising vehicle the unique institution of religious community can provide to facilitate rich intercultural exchange. Our novice director, Brother Joseph Kaganda, invited me to offer a retreat to eight young men completing their year at Saka, a volcanic lake tucked beneath the Ruwenzori mountains in the west of Uganda, near the frontier with Congo. Not wishing to hear myself talk, and realizing that they were used to directed retreats, I offered a morning reflection on the portion of Luke given us to pray with that day, and spent a half hour with each of them in the afternoon. So it was their retreat and my learning experience. I have followed them in their theological study in Nairobi, as we celebrated their final vows in August 2011. It is uncanny how an experience like this can allow privileged access to the lives of others as this *muzungu* (Western white person) came to appreciate the contours of their lives, often violently disrupted. A cultural eye-opener one could never have contrived!

Our predecessors had taken a bold step a quarter of a century ago, when we invited indigenous young men and women into Holy Cross. Joining forces with other missionary groups, they formed two consortia: one in Jinja, Uganda (Philosophy Center-Jinja) for undergraduate work for candidates for Holy Cross, and the other in Nairobi, Kenya (Tangaza College) for theological or professional studies for those who completed the novitiate in Saka as vowed members of the congregation. The result is that our young people receive a superior education, whether in line for ordination or not, with a faculty drawn form different cultures and exhibiting worldwide experience. When I tried to congratulate one of our men who helped carry out this initiative, with little funds and much faith, he would only say: "Hell, we couldn't homeschool them!" That is the missionary spirit I so admire and have finally become a small part of. What is more, intercultural exchange in Holy Cross is enhanced by gender complementarity, in the original vision of our nineteenth-century founder, Basil Moreau—a microcosm of church (and of humanity): lay and clerical, male and female.

So I can only be grateful that two-thirds of the life and times elaborated here have been lived out in this congregation, and that I now find myself stimulated by students and colleagues at Tangaza. The imaginative vision of distinguished Holy Cross confreres, including Bill Blum, CSC, stands at the inception of the collaborative venture that is Tangaza College, soon to become Tangaza-Consolata University. In the meantime, the leader of the initial Holy Cross group, Vincent McCauley, CSC, once made bishop of Fort Portal in western Uganda, directed his efficacious vision to expanding Gaba Seminary (in Kampala) for the Ugandan bishops. In the wake of Vatican II, he resigned in favor of an African, and was quickly selected to be general secretary of the bishops' conference of East Africa, in whose name he founded the Catholic University of East Africa. The journey from Council Bluffs, Iowa, into Holy Cross, and thence to Bangladesh and East Africa, has been admirably captured by Richard Gribble in *Vincent McCauley, C.S.C.: Bishop of the Poor, Apostle of East Africa* (2008). To find myself also teaching in the institution he inspired, adjacent to Tangaza in Nairobi, can only enhance this stage of my own journey.

The Great Lakes Region of Africa

The original East African community is currently expanding to include a Rwanda restored after the tragic genocide of the 1990s, as well as neighboring Burundi—both originally francophone. Adjoining the Democratic Republic of Congo, this Great Lakes region continues to experience devastating civil conflict, aggravated by systematic rape of its women—all in the name of ethnic conflict yet focused on exploiting Congo mineral wealth. My relationship with David Tshimba led us to participate in a creative response in faith to this dire situation, inspired by an old friend, Emmanuel Katongole. The gathering took place in 2011 at Gaba Seminary outside Kampala, with some seventy intent and faith-filled peacemakers from seven African countries (eleven countries in all), who came together to pray and delineate strategies towards peace that would also be transforming. For these strategies would have to body forth a "new creation" if the dire trajectories for the Great Lakes region of Africa are to be turned around. Indeed, these people, young and old, knew that, for they have suffered through it—from northern Uganda to eastern Congo and southern Sudan. Talking, singing, praying, and eating were carried on together, clearing hearts from preconceptions and false expectations, to give way to hope. Sponsored by the Duke Center for Faith and Reconciliation, directed by Emmanuel Katongole and Chris Rice, and supported by Christian groups in Africa and worldwide, the gathering exceeded an academic conference, as the call of peacemaking demands more than analytic skills. Its five days fairly epitomized my own attempt to give thanks to the God who has directed my life though such parlous times and places, while crowning these puny efforts with that unmistakable note of joy that suffuses Africans whose lot has been one of suffering.

This charismatic meeting offered a serendipitous microcosm of church in Africa. But where is church going? What sorts of leaders will emerge? What about lay voices? These questions will continue; much depends on the "church" in question, and the gathering just described was blessedly ecumenical—exceptional, as we have noted, for Uganda. The Catholic community seems to be quite dominated by a clerical caste, though filled with willing and eager laypersons, older and younger. One of our confreres, Fred Jenga, CSC, directs a family ministry program (sponsored internationally by Holy Cross) directed towards young people, and has trained a cadre of peer ministers to serve them. He finds a hunger that standard church life does little to slake, but has shown a way to serve young people in the process. So, as is always the case with "church" in whatever region (or era), initiatives can be found that are heartening, along with practices that are debilitating. Only the future will tell; but again, I find the spirit and initiative of our young Holy Cross men and women in East Africa to be at once heartening and stimulating.

From Colonial to Postcolonial: How Africa Can Enlighten Us about "the Enlightenment" and Israel/Palestine

Working and teaching in East Africa has also awakened me from what remained of my Western myopia, a weaning begun in Rome to continue into the eastern Mediterranean, to South and West Asia, now culminating in sub-Saharan Africa. Living in each of these worlds elicits the need for a set of tools to deconstruct Western fascination with "the Enlightenment." The work of a Ugandan colleague, Emmanuel Katongole, had alerted me to Adam Hochschild's startling exposé of colonial rapacity, *King Leopold's*

Ghost. An invitation to Saint Paul's in London (for a conference on science and religion) led me into that exquisite church for evensong. Startled at the contrast between the elegantly plain nave and the ornate choir where we were seated, quick dating reminded me forcibly: ornate, of course, due to the slave trade. That sudden awakening revealed the seamy underside of what we celebrate as "the Enlightenment." Indeed, of the dirty little secret: the Enlightenment justified colonization while the outcomes of colonizing bankrolled the Enlightenment.

Yet I had to become resident in Uganda before all that dawned on me, even though I had recognized long before that the secret of the State of Israel lay in its being a colony of world Jewry, and one that snuck in, so to speak, at the advent of decolonization, due to the outpouring of sympathy when Hitler's camps were opened. So the godfather of the State of Israel turns out to be none other than Adolph Hitler, whose diabolical plot to purify a conquered Europe of Jews expedited UN approval of a colony on someone else's land, as it would prove to poison Israeli politics ever since. So an awareness born in Israel/Palestine and brought suddenly to light in Saint Paul's Cathedral, has been clinched in Uganda. Once we allow ourselves to be brought up short critically, we will never cease to learn. So to those who ask me what it is like to be in Africa, I cannot help responding: Africa does not exist; it was "discovered" by Europeans in 1884 at the Conference of Berlin, to be carved up and exploited. I have been welcomed in Uganda, part of East Africa, also carved up and exploited, yet now a region in its own right, however artificially conceived.

Promising vistas now open up through participating in the life of theological inquiry at Tangaza College in Nairobi, soon to become Tangaza Consolata University, and philosophical life of the adjoining Catholic University of East Africa. Moreover, Nairobi brings me closer to Tanzania, where I have been asked to assist a student at Saint Augustine's University in Mwonza, to complete her dissertation for Margaret Beaufort Institute in Cambridge. Those acquainted with the postcolonial history of East Africa cannot but be stirred by Julius Nyrere's bold initiatives that issued in Tanzanians' identifying with their country—a rare phenomenon in either Kenya or Uganda. Indeed, my fascination with that singular development in these artificial countries still bound to tribal differences, has stimulated my desire to attain a working grasp of Swahili, in order to move into that new terrain. We shall see, but the guiding hand of Providence has prevailed thus far!